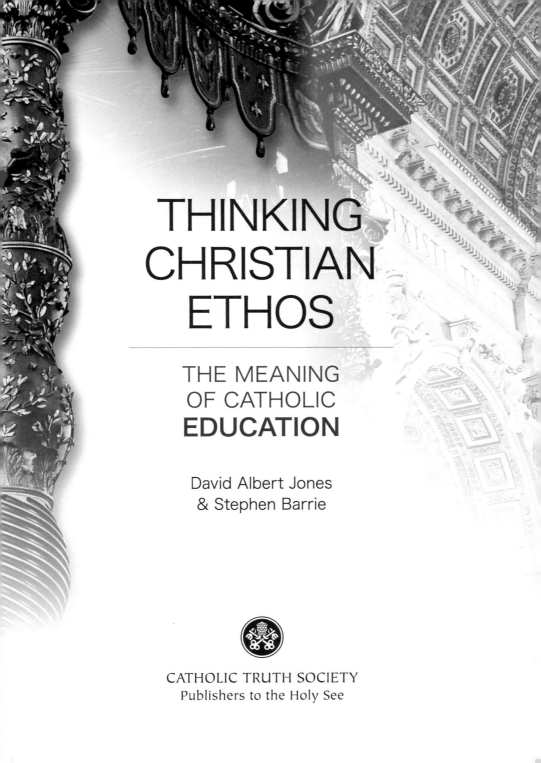

THINKING CHRISTIAN ETHOS

THE MEANING OF CATHOLIC **EDUCATION**

David Albert Jones
& Stephen Barrie

CATHOLIC TRUTH SOCIETY
Publishers to the Holy See

CTS Publications

CTS booklets explain the faith, teaching and life of the Catholic Church. They are based on Sacred Scripture, the Second Vatican Council documents, and the *Catechism of the Catholic Church*. Our booklets provide authentic Catholic teaching; they address issues of life and of truth which are relevant to all. They aim to inform and educate readers on the many issues that people have to deal with today.

In addition, CTS nurtures and supports the Christian life through its many spiritual, liturgical, educational and pastoral books. As Publisher to the Holy See, CTS publishes the official documents of the Catholic Church as they are issued.

website: CTSbooks.org

Original English edition:
© 2015 by David Albert Jones and Stephen Barrie, Oxford, England

Nihil Obstat: Reverend Jonathan Veasey STL (Censor)
Imprimatur: Bernard Longley, Archbishop, Archdiocese of Birmingham, 10th March 2015.

The *Nihil Obstat* and *Imprimatur* are a declaration that a publication is considered to be free from doctrinal or moral error. It is not implied that those who have granted the Nihil Obstat and Imprimatur agree with the contents, opinions or statements expressed.

Layout and design, Catholic Truth Society, London, England

Cover image: Detail of the baldachin and interior of the Saint Peter Cathedral in Vatican, Rome, Italy. St. Peter's Basilica © Cesc Assawin / Shutterstock.com.

2015 (English language edition) published by Incorporated Catholic Truth Society, London.

ISBN 978 1 78469 031 1

Contents

Acknowledgments

There are a great many people to thank for their support and help with what has been a relatively long and collaborative project. A draft text for Thinking Christian Ethos was revised in the light of a wide consultation process involving a conference held in Oxford in 2011 and both general and targeted invitations to teachers, governors, school chaplains and others with a stake in Catholic education. These invitations generated dozens of responses expressing a wealth of experience. We are grateful to all of those who participated in this process. These are too numerous to name individually but we must at least make mention of John Hussey (Principal), Clare Haly (Head of Religious Studies) and Catherine Enticknap (Lay Chaplain) at Saint Gregory the Great Catholic School, Oxford, which not only hosted the 2011 conference but also actively engaged with the whole process. Catherine Enticknap also helped further in particular with reflections on how teachers and school chaplains might make use of each of the chapters. We are also grateful to Blackfriars Hall, Oxford for hosting a number of seminars and meetings. The consultation process was coordinated primarily by Stephen Barrie. After the consultation responses were collated and addressed the text went through several further iterations as a result of internal and external feedback. Most of the initial drafting of this book was done by David Albert Jones with comments from Stephen Barrie who also drafted an introduction and parts of chapter 9. The material for chapter 7 is drawn principally from Fr Andrew Pinsent and Fr Marcus Holden *Lumen: The Catholic Gift to Civilisation* and is used with permission (though it should be noted that this material has been rewritten with a number of additions and readers should consult the original text before attributing any statement in this book to the authors of *Lumen*). We are grateful to the Catholic Truth Society for expressing interest in this project from the outset, and for all the work they have done on design. This project would not have been possible without generous grants from two charitable trusts Culham St Gabriel's and another educational trust. Finally no acknowledgement in a Catholic document should be complete without acknowledgement of the One from whom all things come and on whose grace we all depend, for 'If the Lord does not build the house, in vain do its builders labour' (Psalm 127:1).

Authors

Prof David Albert Jones MA (Cantab) MA MSt DPhil (Oxon) FHEA is the Director of the Anscombe Bioethics Centre, Oxford, Research Fellow in Bioethics at Blackfriars Hall, Oxford, and Visiting Professor at St Mary's University, Twickenham.

Mr Stephen Barrie BA(Hons) MA is Education Officer at the Anscombe Bioethics Centre and is studying for a PhD in Philosophy at King's College, London.

Introduction

'Every education teaches a philosophy; if not by dogma then by suggestion, by implication, by atmosphere. Every part of that education has a connection with every other part. If it does not all combine to convey some general view of life it is not an education at all.' G.K. Chesterton *The Common Man* page 166.

This book is about the meaning of Catholic education. It is not a book only for practising Roman Catholics but is a resource for anyone who wishes to explore how education is to be understood from a Christian perspective. It sets out a vision of education that is, or that ought to be, embodied in a Church School (especially but not only in a Catholic school). Its primary concern is religious and moral education, not only as subjects in themselves, but as the foundation of the entire educational process.

The project, of which this book is the centre-piece, grew out of the experience of the authors, and in particular from their discussions with students, teachers and school leaders. A school's 'ethos' is notoriously tricky to pin down, and while lists of attributes or values may indicate a general direction, it can be hard to see where these lists come from, what they might mean in practice, or what unites them. For a Church School there is the additional question of what, if anything, is distinctive about this list. How is it any different to what would be said of any good school?

We hope that this book is useful not only as background reading that addresses these questions, but also for teachers in lesson and assembly planning, for school leaders in planning staff development and INSET days and for general readers interested in the educational traditions of the Christian Church. Each chapter begins with some pointers to possible use of the material, together with a cross-curricular guide showing some of the links between the themes of this book and various AS/A level religious studies and philosophy curricula (OCR Religious Studies, AQA Religious Studies, AQA Philosophy and Edexcel Religious Studies).

For more detail of the requirements of the Catholic Church in relation to Catholic schools, for example in the appointment of members of the governing body and key posts, readers should consult Mgr Marcus Stock's *Christ at the Centre: Why the Church Provides Catholic Schools* (CTS, 2012). This also provides valuable statements of the fundamental characteristics of Catholic schools and the outward signs of a Catholic school's ethos. There are also a number of scholarly monographs, collected volumes, and entire journals devoted to the topic of Catholic education, some of which are referred to in the bibliography and recommendations for further reading included at the end of this book.

The aim of *Thinking Christian Ethos* is to complement these resources by exploring in a systematic and accessible way the worldview needed to sustain a Catholic understanding of education. Its focus is reflection on the aim of education in general and of Christian education in particular. These reflections are practical because the first step in any practical activity is to ask what we are aiming to achieve. The book aims to provide a general background to understanding the way the Christian faith, and in particular the Catholic Church, relates to education in schools; it is not written as a textbook or teaching aid, but we hope the curriculum references providing links between themes and topics in the curriculum will prove useful. It is also important to note that parts of this book will support and complement teaching across the whole school, not just in RE and philosophy classes.

As a whole, the book is based on the premise that a closer acquaintance with the ideas that have guided the Church in the past (i.e. the intellectual tradition of the Church, in particular the 'three As': Aristotle, Augustine, and Aquinas) will enrich teaching and learning across the curriculum, even in subjects not normally associated with the school's ethos. Acquaintance with the Catholic tradition can enrich the school life in this way because it sheds light both on the nature of education and on distinctive features of the Christian life. We cannot claim to have provided a check-list for Christian ethos, but we do hope that progressing through the chapters of this book will provide an outline and a reflective account or 'apologia': tracing the thinking behind a Christian ethos, correcting some myths historically associated with Catholic education, and providing the basis for on-going discussion and study.

Before considering what, if anything, Christianity has to offer to education, we start by asking a more general question. What is the point of education? What are we aiming to achieve? A number of years ago the then Secretary of State for education, Charles Clarke, dismissed 'education for its own sake' as 'a bit dodgy'. It is not only politicians and businesses but workers' organisations, professional bodies, parents and students themselves who often demand that education should help students find suitable employment. However, the notion that the needs of the economy should dictate the kind of education children receive is a problematic one. How are we supposed to predict the needs of economy in ten, or twenty, or thirty years' time? In many cases children will in the future be doing jobs that have not even been invented yet. More fundamentally, a focus only on economic activity excludes much of what makes life worth living, and indeed of what makes society possible.

Education helps prepare young people for adult life, and so it raises the deeper question of what human life is about, what makes a good or worthwhile life. This in turn raises the question of how we understand ourselves. Whether or not it is recognised explicitly, education always presupposes a particular concept of what it means to be a human person. Before we are able to say what it is for a person to be well-formed or prepared for life, we need to think about what it is for a human person to be at all. What kind of being is a human being?

The first part of this book, which is about the aim or meaning of education in general, thus starts with a discussion of what it is to be a human person (chapter 1) before moving on to the integral formation of human persons (chapter 2) which will form the basis of an understanding of the aims and ethos of education (chapter 3). This section draws heavily on the thought on Aristotle (d. 322 BCE), because in the view of the authors (and much of the Western philosophical and ethical tradition) Aristotle had quite a lot of good ideas! The way in which Aristotle is used in these chapters

St Gregory the Great, Roman Catholic Secondary School

also draws on the thirteenth century Dominican friar Thomas Aquinas (d. 1274), and on his twentieth century fellow-Dominican Fr Herbert McCabe (d. 2001). Again, this is because they understood, communicated, and developed Aristotle's thought so well, and added a few good ideas of their own.

The first three chapters include occasional references to Christian doctrine, but not as the basis for their key conclusions. The arguments which are presented do not rely on a specifically Christian worldview. Rather, the chapters develop a worldview that is sufficiently human to be open to religion. The second part of the book asks what difference, if any, Christianity adds to this human vision of education. Chapter 4 focuses on Jesus, and how to understand him if we believe that God sent him

Fr Herbert McCabe OP

into the world. Chapter 5 sets out the implications of this Christian vision for how we understand and cultivate the virtues. Chapter 6 sets out some of the implications for education. The Christian religion is not simply another way to communicate ethical values that are, at root, common to humanity. Rather, Christianity transforms our understanding of life, virtues and thus of the task of education. In particular, it adds an acknowledgement of human weakness together with a sense of hope that is not given by pagan philosophers such as Aristotle. In these chapters and in the following three chapters it is the fifth century bishop Augustine of Hippo (d. 430) who is our main guide to the significance of Jesus, the nature of the Church, and the meaning of the Christian Scriptures. This is in part because Augustine remains arguably the most influential theologian for Western Christianity after the Apostles, both in Catholic and in Reformed communities. He is taken as a guide also, and more importantly, because his theological insights remain profound, not least for education.

The last three chapters apply this perspective to a school setting, and especially to a Church School. Chapter 7 explores the impact of Christianity on Western culture and thus on all the different academic disciplines. Chapter 8 explores the nature and ethos of a Catholic School. It ends with a reflection on the significance of a Christian worldview for the curriculum. Chapter 9 describes the mission of the school to the world. It shows how being more distinctively Christian should encourage greater engagement with the world, inspired by Christian faith, hope, and charity. The culmination of this final chapter, and thus the book, is a reflection on the aims of education from a Christian perspective. It relates the integral formation of the person to the person of Jesus Christ, the beginning and end of Catholic education.

1. The Nature of Education,
What is needed for human persons to flourish?

1. Human Persons

Some pointers for making use of this chapter

This first chapter may be useful for reference when giving assemblies and lessons on what it is to be human, a human person. The chapter links in with a theme continually referred to in meditation, prayer, assembly/liturgies and para-liturgies which is the human person as made in the image of God (Genesis 1:27). The theme of humans being made in the image of God is taken up more explicitly in chapter 9 of this book, but the present chapter contains a reflection on what is distinctive about human life. Young people need affirmation and support in building healthy self-esteem and self-worth based on a realistic premise (not on empty hopes or on the encouragement of vanity). In addition to telling students that, when God made the whole world including human beings, it was 'very good' (Genesis 1:31), it may also be useful to introduce the term 'person'. It is hoped that the clarification of that term given here may be helpful, both for what it affirms and for exposing misguided ideas about what makes someone a person. Finally, friendships and the challenges they present to many young people create a constant need for pastoral counsel and circle time discussion. The ending of this chapter provides material for reflection not only for chaplaincy departments but also for tutors.

Curriculum Links

OCR

RS Unit G572: AS Religious Ethics (Natural Law, Religious Ethics, Applied Ethics)

RS Unit G575: AS Developments in Christian Theology (Human Nature)

RS Unit G581: A2 Philosophy of Religion (Life and Death: The Soul)

RS Unit G582: A2 Religious Ethics (Virtue Ethics)

AQA

AQA RS AS Unit A Religion and Ethics 1 (RSS01) (Nature and Value of Human Life)

AQA RS AS Unit B Religion and Ethics 2 (RSS02) (Natural Law)

Philosophy Unit 1 PHIL1 An Introduction to Philosophy 1 (Persons)

Edexcel

AS Unit 1 Area B (Ethics, Concepts and Dilemmas)

AS Unit 2 Area C (The Study of Ethics, Medical Ethics, the Natural World)

A2 Unit 3 Area B (Natural Moral Law, Virtue Ethics, Justice)

A2 Unit 4 Question 2 (Ethics), Question 4 (Christianity)

What are we?

The purpose of education is to help young people grow and develop to fulfil their potential, to be all they can be. Therefore, education presupposes some idea of the aim or meaning of human life, what human life is about, what it is for us to flourish or excel at being human. Going deeper, if we are to discover what fulfils human beings we need to understand what *kind* of beings we are.

One answer to this question is to say that what is most important to us is that we are *persons*: we are not only things and not only animals of a peculiar kind (animals that walk upright and that wear clothes). We have a life that means something to us, that is personal. As human persons we relate to one another as 'you' and 'me' and 'us'. I am not just an 'it'. I am a 'who'. To recognise this is to recognise our common dignity, a dignity shared by every human being. If we want to understand what we should be aiming at in educating young people, then we need to understand what it is to be a human person.

There is a danger here, however, that we might try to run before we can walk. We might try jumping straight to being a person and forget that we are also physical beings and animals of a specific kind, even if we are more than this. Human persons are not angels or ghosts. Rather, we live a life that is at once personal and bodily. This is not only something that a secular philosopher or a scientist might recognise. It is also an important part of Christian doctrine as is evident, for example, in a statement of Christian belief from the middle ages.

> We firmly believe and openly confess that there is only one true God, eternal and immense, omnipotent, unchangeable, incomprehensible, and ineffable… who from the beginning of time and by his omnipotent power made from nothing creatures both spiritual and corporeal, angelic, namely, and mundane, and then human, as it were, common, composed of spirit and body. (Creed of Lateran IV, 1215)

Human beings are composed of spirit and body. We are a specific kind of physical being. When considering physical beings we can always ask what they are made of (their material composition) and what specific shape they have, or what kind of thing they are (their form). These days people are used to thinking that what matters is matter, the stuff something is made from, whereas form is a mere formality, a mere re-arrangement of the atoms or molecules. This might be true of something like a statue, which was one of the examples Aristotle used to illustrate the distinction between

matter and form: wood is the matter, and the shape given to it by the carpenter is its form. The wood does seem to matter more, and the form is whatever the carpenter happens to carve. However, from the perspective of biology, form is more important than matter. If a cat dies its weight does not change, nor the chemical composition of its body (though this will start to change very rapidly), but almost everything interesting about the cat has been destroyed. It no longer

catches mice or generates kittens. It no longer pounces or purrs. It is no longer a living being or a member of a particular animal species. The cat is no more. It is an ex-cat. The dead cat is not a cat at all but is only the physical remains of what was once a cat.

From the perspective of biology, then, what something is, essentially, is much more to do with its form than with its matter. This is also the case in modern physics, where atoms are not thought of as solid lumps of matter, tiny billiard balls moved by external forces. Rather matter is thought of in terms of probability clouds that are constituted by waveforms within fields of force. This is important because it reminds us that we need to understand human beings in relation to a particular *form* of life. We are not simply reducible to the stuff of which we are made: the whole is more than the sum of its parts. Our material composition changes all the time as we eat, drink, breathe, sweat and go to the toilet. Matter goes in and matter goes out but we are the same living being because we have an enduring dynamic source of life from within.

This is the first important thing to say about human persons, and thus about the education of human persons. We are beings of a particular kind and we have a particular form that is our nature. It is for this reason that some things will be good for human beings (such as education, creativity, friendship) and some things will harm human beings (such as ignorance, monotony, isolation). We have a specific nature and there will be activities and environments that fit with this nature and complete it and others that will harm it. Nurture builds on and presupposes this specific nature.

Education presupposes that human beings have a specific form, a human nature which is completed by nurture. However, the very idea of nurture also implies that human nature is not something static like the form of a statue or a painting. It is the nature of human beings to be changing constantly and human persons come to maturity through a process involving many changes. Our nature is the nature of a living thing that grows and develops.

Living & growing

Human beings are not only physical beings with a specific form (like stars or crystals) but belong to that most interesting category of physical beings, those that are alive. One of the earliest books on the nature of living things, which is still well worth reading, was written by Aristotle in the fourth century before the common era. He called it, 'On the soul' (and it is sometimes known by its Latin name, *De Anima*).

By 'soul' he meant what animates living things so that they are distinct from non-living things. Aristotle thought that we recognise something as alive because it is not only moved from outside (as leaves are blown by the wind or rain falls downwards) but, in a certain way, is able to move itself. He did not mean that living things must be able to move about. Growth is already a kind of motion (as can be seen if we speed it up by time-lapse photography). Rocks and stones are worn down or moved about by forces outside themselves, by the wind and the rain, by ice, and sometimes by the growth

Growth is already a kind of motion

17

of plants or the movement of animals. But they do not move themselves. In contrast, even though plants do not move themselves from place to place, they grow due to a source and pattern of movement from within. That is why each kind of plant develops in ways characteristic of its kind. Its roots grow down, its stems grow upwards, its buds open, its leaves turn toward the sun, and the roots, stems, buds and leaves have a shape characteristic of its species.

We are all aware that words can be used in different but related senses. When I say that I love my mother and that I love ice-cream, I am not using the word 'love' in exactly the same sense. On the other hand it is not simply a pun (like the cross-eyed teacher who cannot control his pupils). The word 'love' is being used in slightly different senses which are related by analogy. Similarly, when we say that a tiger is alive and a tulip is alive, we are not saying the same thing in both cases, but neither are we engaging in mere wordplay. Whatever is alive has, at some level, the power to move itself and is not purely at the mercy of outside forces. The tulip may not be able to leap about and kill antelope like the tiger, but as it grows from a bulb, flowers, reproduces and returns to a dormant state each year, it is clearly self-moving (or, if you prefer, self-changing) in a way that a rock is not.

Something that can move itself is, literally, an *automobile* – a self-mover. However, it is extremely important to understand that what Americans *call* automobiles are nothing of the kind. They only appear to move themselves. It might seem to someone who saw a car for the first time that it was a living thing, but even our language suggests that we know this is not really the case. If you emerge from your front door one morning to find your car parked on the opposite side of the road from where you left it, you would probably say, not 'My car has moved', but, 'My car has been moved' or, 'Someone has moved my car.'

A crucial difference between tigers and cars is whether the whole comes first or its parts. The tiger is a natural unit and a car is not. When a tiger moves something takes place within its brain which moves another part of it – its legs. It is the tiger as a whole that moves. Its organs – brain, nerves, muscles, joints, legs and so forth – function as parts of the tiger. The tiger comes first, as it were. Its parts are secondary and they are changing all the time. Another way to see this is to ask where cars or tigers come from. Cars are manufactured from parts. They are made by people according to a design created by people for the sake of people. Tigers are not manufactured but are generated by other tigers, their parents, according to a 'design' that is not something separate from them but is their own nature. The word 'nature' simply means what an animal is born with, the inherent form that it has from its origin that is expressed in how it grows, develops, and behaves.

It is because life is movement from within and tends towards a characteristic pattern that each living thing has its own goals or finality, and this is seen by the way that living beings thrive or wither, flourish or decline. Only what is living can flourish. Of course, when we are speaking about tulips or tigers or human beings we are using the word 'life' in different senses, and so what it means for this life to 'flourish' will also be different. However, for every kind of life it makes sense to ask whether it is flourishing, and whether it has what it needs to flourish. In contrast cars may perform well (if they are well-maintained) but they do not blossom or flourish or thrive. They are inanimate. People can flourish and so we can ask what is needed for us to flourish.

This has important implications for education. Education is directed ultimately at what makes for the human flourishing of the person being educated and not only at what makes the person useful for something or to someone else (as a machine is valued only for its use). Similarly, education should never be regarded as a purely mechanical process analogous to manufacturing. There will be elements of education that require practice and repetition but fundamentally education exists to assist the specific growth and development of a human person. Growth and development are activities of the living being, not merely mechanical processes. This is true of all living beings and is even more so in the case of human persons who, among animals, have the supreme capacity to be active and self-directed. Tigers cannot reflect on what they might do in life, whereas human beings by nature ask questions of themselves. Education consists in enabling, supporting and drawing out (ex-ducere) the active human curiosity, which is a power from within.

Feeling & thinking

Education is a distinctive characteristic of human life. Birds imitate one another and many animals learn from their parents how to hunt or what to be wary of, but there is no parallel in the rest of the animal kingdom to the extraordinary investment human communities make in educating their young. This in part is a reflection of how long it takes for human beings to grow up; that is, to become mature and more independent. Indeed, there is a sense in which human beings never grow up, in that we can continue to learn and to grow throughout life. There is always more to learn.

The phenomenon of education therefore raises the question of what is distinctive of human life over and against the life of other animals. However, before looking at what is distinctive we need to see what is common: what we have in common with other animals. Cats, and animals more generally, do not respond to the world only by the slow-motion of growth and development. They move rapidly in response to a perception of their environment. To be an animal is to have one or more of the 'five senses': touch, taste, smell, hearing and sight, and to be able to react to what is sensed.

Animals, as distinct from plants, are defined by their possession of sensation and behaviour. The most basic of the senses and, according to Aristotle, the one that is common to all animals, is the sense of touch by which even simple animals feel their way. Even in the simplest animals there is a tendency to move towards what is perceived as attractive and to move away from what is perceived as noxious. More complex animals not only have more sophisticated senses so that they hear or see distant objects but, more importantly, they have a more sophisticated repertoire of behaviour. In warm-blooded animals this generally includes nurturing behaviour and in many animals it includes complex social behaviours. Higher animals (especially mammals) generally need to bond with their young and, in some species, with a mate and, in some species, with an extended social group. In addition to simple behaviour of seeking what is attractive and avoiding what is repellent, higher animals also need to be able to show aggression in the face of a present threat or flight from the prospect of future danger as well as a range of emotions necessary for social interaction. Hence non-human animals may experience a wide range of emotions including desire, fear, hope, anger and even loneliness.

In the seventeenth century some scientists and philosophers believed that non-human animals were mere automata and they could not feel pain or pleasure, but this was a mistake based on bad philosophy. It was based on the idea that animals are like machines, but this is to put the cart before the horse (quite literally!) Machines are like animals because they have form and function, but the form and function of machines is due to human design and for the sake of human life.  Machines are made by human animals and their form is related to the life of human animals. In contrast animals (all animals) have their own lives and each has a form that is essential to it. The emotional life of animals is a consequence of the way in which they are able to perceive the world and are inclined to react to it. It is a consequence of having tendencies or instincts that are part of their nature. We could, in a poetic manner, compare a dog seeing a stick and a camera 'seeing' a stick when we use it to take a photograph, and we could even make some simplistic comparisons between the components of a camera and the parts of the dog's eye. The difference is that the dog is affected by the stick in a way that the camera is not (and cannot be). The stick has no *meaning* for the camera because

 the camera is not capable of discerning meaning (a human looking through the viewfinder does that). In contrast, the appearance of the stick does not simply remain projected upon the dog's retina as if the eye were a component of a machine. The eye is an organ of the whole dog, so the stick is perceived by the dog himself and has a particular meaning for him (sticks mean fun).

When a dog sees a juicy steak, unless he is ill or has just eaten, he will tend to eat it. He cannot but perceive the steak except under the appearance of something desirable. The steak as perceived is relevant to him; it has a meaning that affects the way the dog behaves, or is inclined to behave if he is not constrained. In contrast if a human being sees the steak she may eat it, but it is just as likely that she will not eat it. Her reasons for not eating the steak can be almost infinite in number. It may belong to someone else, be past its sell-by date, or be earmarked for tonight's supper. She may disapprove of the slaughter of animals for food, have high cholesterol, or prefer to delay eating it until a time when she knows she will enjoy it more. Furthermore if she decides to eat it she will first consider how she wishes it to be cooked (or perhaps whether to have it uncooked as sashimi or as steak tartare). Not only can she have any of these reasons for eating or not eating or eating in a certain way, she can express them in language. Her actions will be determined not only by her feelings but also by her thoughts, and this gives her a degree of freedom not possessed in the same way by other animals. The dog may not eat the steak, of course, but it is likely that this will be because he is well-trained. The steak is on the kitchen table and he knows that he is 'not allowed' in the kitchen. But if this is the case then the reasons for the dog not eating the steak are not those of the dog but those of the dog's owner.

Human beings thus possess a power or powers beyond those of other animals. It might be thought that education, being distinctive of human life, is therefore concerned exclusively with these powers: with thought, with language and knowledge, with the exercise of free will, and not with feelings or emotions. However to think this would be a mistake. While human thinking opens up a whole world of possibilities to us, human persons are still animals and still continue to perceive the world in emotional as well as intellectual terms. An important element of education is, in fact, the integration of these aspects of our personality so that our emotional life is informed by our understanding of where our true good lies. How this may be achieved is the topic of the second chapter of this book, which introduces the concept of good dispositions of character. Throughout this book the word will be used in this specific sense: a disposition is an acquired inclination to act and to react in certain ways.

> A disposition is an acquired inclination to act and to react in certain ways.

Dispositions can inform our emotional life and they can be informed by our thoughts and decisions. Dispositions therefore play an important role in mediating between thoughts and feelings and hence an important role in achieving that integral formation that is the aim of moral education. The need for such dispositions is due to the nature of human persons first as being animals with a rich emotional life and second as being distinctive among animals in their possession of thought and language.

Society, history & education

The radical distinctiveness of human life is also evident in the nature of human society. Some animals, such as tigers and armadillos, are solitary. Others such as sheep and elephants are gregarious (meaning 'of the herd'). The life of human persons is not only gregarious in this sense but is also linguistic and cultural. Other social animals live in herds, groups, or colonies that are characteristic of their species. These social forms are stable across time because they are written into the nature the animals inherit as part of their physical make up. In contrast, human communities constitute a society, a form of social life that is shaped by culture, law, or custom, and is constantly refashioned by debate, disagreement, reform, or revolution. This cultural inheritance is something that is changeable and varies with time and place, just as language changes over time and there are different languages spoken in different places. Another way to say this is to say, as Aristotle said, that we are *political* animals.

It is only in human political societies that history is possible. We could tell a story about European society, taking as our starting point the slave-owning Roman Empire, and talking about the debates and movements along the way, the influence of religious faith and political ideologies, the advances and the false starts, as well as the threats of reactionary movements like National Socialism in the 1930s: we could construct a narrative that would bring us to the present day where slavery, if not actually vanished from Europe, is at least illegal and publically condemned. It is not possible to tell a similar story about other animal species.

We do try to tell stories about other animal communities over time, but they always end up being one of three things. They are either (1) descriptions of evolution, which is a biological response of a species to circumstances, not circumstances animals create deliberately or seek to influence, or (2) stories about the human manipulation of other animals, e.g. changing their behaviour through domestication, hunting, or destruction of their habitat, or (3) a kind of fiction (like *Animal Farm* or *Watership Down*) which seems to be about pigs, dogs, or rabbits, but is really about human beings in the guise of nonhuman animals.

As human society is by its nature historical, so each human person is also a character in a larger story (actually in lots of stories). If we observe a man digging a hole we can imagine a variety of possible answers to the question, 'What is he doing?' We can see that any of these answers will involve the telling of a story, or a part of a story. In attributing his behaviour to planting potatoes in preparation for winter we will be telling a horticultural story, while in ascribing his behaviour to taking exercise or pleasing his wife, we will be telling a domestic story. Perhaps he is hiding something in the garden: this may be innocent or it may be criminal. Perhaps he is seeking to grow vegetables as a political statement against the power of supermarkets. Every human being inhabits multiple narratives — professional, social, domestic, sexual, spiritual, mercantile, intellectual, cultural and so forth — and these narratives inevitably overlap.

'a story in search of a narrator' Paul Ricoeur

Human life itself, as Paul Ricoeur beautifully observed, is a 'story in search of a narrator'. As we grow and develop we find ourselves within a story that is already ongoing, the history of human society, or at least that part of history and that part of society in the time and place where we grow up. It is only by education, in the broadest sense, that we are introduced to this world, to this history and society, and it is education that enables us (or should enable us) to begin to live our own story. In this sense, we are not only human beings, but human *becomings*. A human being can be responsible for her life in a radically different way from, for example, a dog. This is not true of every human being, or of any human being at every stage of life, but it is characteristic of a mature human being. An important task of education is to help young people realise their capacity to influence, or even substantially to alter, their own life stories through the decisions they make and by the kind of person each one becomes.

Persons, dignity & friendship

To recap: Human beings are physical beings with a certain inherent form that determines our nature. More specifically we are living beings, and as such it is in our nature to be active and to develop and flourish in certain ways over time. Human beings are animals and the world is meaningful to us in an animal way, through sensations and emotional inclinations which we need to integrate as we develop to maturity. Finally we are rational animals: our ability to think about things and communicate those thoughts through language makes us radically different from all other animals, or at least from all those animals with which we are familiar. This radical difference is evident at some times more than others, and in very young people, and very ill people, and people who are asleep, it might not be evident at all. However, though we are not always thinking we are always animals of a kind that, as a species, is capable of thought. This is what Aristotle meant when he said that human beings are by nature 'rational animals'.

> The word 'soul' refers to the principle of life, the form or actual organisation of a living being.

The word 'soul' refers to the principle of life, the form or actual organisation of a living being. Those living beings who are persons, who have a nature that includes the capacity for thought and freedom, are said to possess a 'rational soul' (sometimes called a 'spiritual soul'). However it is important to say that each living being has only one life and one principle of life, its soul. The soul of a human person is thus the unifying principle of his or her biological, emotional, and intellectual life.

We are now in a position to reflect on what it is to be a human person (that distinctive characteristic of human life expressed already by reference to our 'linguistic', 'cultural', 'political' or 'rational' nature). Persons are capable by nature of relating to one another as 'I' to 'you'. Human beings are persons in virtue of being, by nature, rational animals. To describe humans as persons is to recognise that human life possesses a capacity for freedom and a special dignity that is worthy of respect. Human society is often flawed by a cult of personality or celebrity and by prejudice against people of low social status. However, there is a fundamental level of respect that is due to everyone simply as a human person. This is the basis of fundamental human rights, and is why these rights are described as 'inalienable'. This inherent dignity is signified by the word 'person'.

> Persons are capable by nature of relating to one another as 'I' to 'you'. Human beings are persons in virtue of being, by nature, rational animals.

Ethics: The concept of 'personhood'

There is a very dangerous move among some modern philosophers (for example, the Australian philosopher Peter Singer) to confine the word 'person' only to individuals who currently have the capacity to express their linguistic or rational nature. Human beings who, through immaturity or disability, are not able to speak or think, or who do not seem to be able to do so, are then relegated to the status of 'human nonpersons'. A 'nonperson' need not be given respect or protection and they may even be killed by abortion, infanticide, or euthanasia if their existence is inconvenient to others. The Catholic philosopher Elizabeth Anscombe (d. 2001) described this move as 'a mere trick' by which 'thinkers trade on the weight of the word "person", although they define it wrongly in terms of characteristics which may come and go and which are a matter of degree'. In contrast she argued that 'A human being is a person because the kind to which he belongs is characterised by a rational nature. Thus we have the same individual, and hence the same person, when we have the same human being'. *(Human Life, Action and Ethics, pages 267-68)*

It is useful to refer to human beings as *persons* to remind ourselves of our inherent dignity possessed by human beings by virtue of the kind of beings we are, and not based on our achievements or on the particular status given to us by society. The word 'person' also calls attention to the characteristic ways that human beings flourish through relationships with other persons. Generally it is through our relationships with others that we learn what it is for us to be persons. Herbert McCabe succinctly observed, 'as knives are for cutting and pens are for writing, people are for living with one another' (*God, Christ and Us*, page 47). Someone might be a good dancer, a good footballer or a good physicist, but what makes that person quite simply good (good at being a human person) is how he or she lives with others. And this human living with each other has a name. We call it friendship. Friendship is more than people wishing well to other people. It involves sharing a common personal life.

'Friendship is necessary to life, since no one would choose to live without friends even if he had all other material goods. Friends are a refuge in times of poverty and misfortune, they help to guard the young from error, they help the old in their weakness, and help those in the prime of life to perform noble actions.' Nichomachean Ethics

As Aristotle puts it, 'Friendship is necessary to life, since no one would choose to live without friends even if he had all other material goods. Friends are a refuge in times of poverty and misfortune, they help to guard the young from error, they help the old in their weakness, and help those in the prime of life to perform noble actions.' *Nichomachean Ethics*, VIII.1.

The word 'friend' is used in many senses for those with whom we are on friendly terms or whose company we find congenial but we are aware of a higher form of friendship that we cannot share with many people. Friendship in its highest or truest sense is shared personal life constituted by an equal and mutual relationship of unselfish love. Aristotle argued that it was not possible to be a true friend to more than a very few people, and perhaps only one. Whatever our views on this, friendship expresses something essential to human life and is an important element in all human flourishing. One way to discover what we need in order to flourish, and therefore understand better *all* our human relationships, is to ask what characteristics we would want in a friend and what characteristics we would want for ourselves in order to be a good friend to another. This is the subject of our next chapter.

> Friendship in its highest or truest sense is shared personal life constituted by an equal and mutual relationship of unselfish love.

2. The Integral Formation of Persons

Some pointers for making use of this chapter

The theme of 'the virtues' is increasingly popular not only within the curriculum but also as an approach to pastoral practice and catechetical assembly programmes. The chaplaincy team may wish to consider whether to make catechesis more directly and explicitly focused on the virtues. This chapter is very applicable to such current developments (especially if used in conjunction with chapter 5). Reflection on the virtues could also be supported through themes in retreat and meditation for both staff and students.

The virtues and vices would also be a possible focus for reconciliation services where these are held for the whole school, or for staff. The idea of conscience is sometimes introduced as early as Primary school so it may be important to revisit it and clarify the scope and implications of the idea. For this purpose the definitions and explanations may be a helpful place to start.

Those delivering sex and relationships education, which is often done in conjunction with Chaplaincy, RE, Science and sometimes external secular agencies (though this can carry certain dangers), would benefit from the reading of the latter pages of this second chapter. These provide a starting point for reflection on what should be the aim of sex and relationships education. Those teaching in this area should also note that the theme will recur in the third chapter where it will be approached from the perspective of the key role of parents in education and the importance of positive collaboration with parents, especially for moral education.

Curriculum Links

OCR

OCR RS Unit G572: AS Religious Ethics (Virtue, Natural Law)

OCR RS Unit G575: AS Developments in Christian Theology (Human Nature, Common Good, Justice)

OCR RS Unit G582: A2 Religious Ethics (Virtue Ethics, Conscience, Applied Ethics)

AQA RS

AQA RS AS Unit A Religion and Ethics 1 (RSS01) (Nature and Value of Human Life)

AQA RS AS Unit B Religion and Ethics 2 (RSS02) (Natural Law, Virtues)

AQA A2 Unit 3A Religion and Ethics (Virtue Ethics)

AQA A2 Unit 4C Topic II Ways of Moral Decision-Making

AQA Philosophy

AQA Philosophy Unit 1 PHIL1 An Introduction to Philosophy 1 (Being moral)

AQA Philosophy Unit 2 PHIL2 An Introduction to Philosophy 2 (Tolerance)

AQA Philosophy Unit 3 PHIL3 Key Themes in Philosophy (Justice, the Common Good, Moral Philosophy, Making Decisions)

Edexcel

A2 Unit 3 Religious Studies — Developments, Area B (Ethics – Virtue Ethics, Justice)

The need for virtue

Teachers generally hope that at least some of their students will listen to what they say, but in relation to moral education, according to Aristotle, 'listening attentively will not make you good'. What else is needed then? As well as passing on knowledge, the role of moral education is to help people cultivate those dispositions of character conducive to fostering friendship and human flourishing: human moral excellences or 'virtues'. A moral virtue is a settled disposition to react in the right way and do the right thing; that is, to do what promotes the true flourishing of human persons. Virtues are dispositions that have to do with practical behaviour. They belong to our living, which is a complex interweaving of feeling and thinking. They come with practice and become a kind of 'second nature'.

Let us take an example. Imagine two university students who each have to write an extended essay as part of their assessment. Peter is worried that he will not pass and so asks Mary if she will write his essay for him. He offers to pay her, which she refuses, but she likes him and feels sorry for him and decides to help. Though at first she intends only to give suggestions and make comments, she finds herself drafting most of the essay. Peter says that he will adapt it, but in the end submits the essay unchanged, passing it off as his own. Mary discovers this, but thinks that she will get into trouble if she admits her involvement, so she remains silent. Both Peter and Mary successfully complete this part of the assessment and pass the course as a whole. Peter is relieved and thinks little of it afterwards but Mary remains troubled by what happened. After the course finishes they do not keep in touch.

> A moral virtue is a settled disposition to react in the right way and do the right thing; that is, to do what promotes the true flourishing of human persons.

In this story Peter and Mary both act badly, though in slightly different ways, and for different reasons. Peter lacks *courage* to rise to the challenge of the assessment and face the risk of failure. He also lacks the virtue of *justice*, in that by dishonesty he puts himself at an unfair advantage over other students. His actions may also be unfair to others in the future, for example if he were to get a job of the basis of his supposed abilities. Finally, he seeks to encourage Mary to do the wrong thing by offering her money. This puts her in a difficult situation, which is unfair to her. Mary does better than Peter. She recognises that what he is suggesting is wrong and she refuses to take any money. However, without sufficient *temperateness* in her emotions Mary's good intentions are undermined by her attraction to Peter and this clouds her *good sense*. She should have recognised that, given her feelings for him, it would be unwise to start 'helping' in this way. Mary also lacks the *courage* needed to face up to what is happening and put a stop to it, or at least own up to it afterwards. Nevertheless, she seems to retain enough inclination to justice to trouble her conscience, whereas Peter seems to have no remorse about cheating. He is certainly in the worse state. It is also noticeable that, while Mary acts out of her attraction to Peter, this does not lead to a lasting friendship. The story is fictional, but it is credible. Partnership in crime is not a secure foundation for friendship.

Four cardinal virtues, L - R: Temperance, Prudence, Fortitude and Justice.

This simple story illustrates four fundamental virtues that we need to cultivate in order to be good: courage, temperateness, justice, and good sense. These are commonly called the 'cardinal virtues', not because they are characteristic of red-cassocked Catholic clerics, but because they are the 'hinges' (in Latin, *cardines*) upon which the door of morality rests and swings. Although we associate talk of the virtues with Aristotle, for example in his *Nicomachean Ethics*, it was in fact his teacher, Plato, who suggested that there were four foundational moral virtues. Thomas Aquinas, building not only on Plato and Aristotle but on later thinkers such as Cicero, Ambrose, and Augustine, was able to provide a more detailed and systematic exposition of these four virtues.

Of course, when Plato formulated the cardinal virtues he was only *discovering* them. He no more invented the virtues than Newton invented gravity. What he understood, in a rudimentary way and long before the dawn of modern psychology, was that what he called 'the soul' has a structure, and that virtue is to the soul what health is to the body. Plato noted that human beings are apt to experience 'inner conflict'. It makes sense to us to say things like 'I have wrestled with my conscience'. For example, upon finding a bundle of banknotes on the pavement, our emotional desires may move us to do one thing (pocket it because it will come in useful), but our reason may move us in the opposite direction (hand it in to the police because it does not belong to me). These are two of the faculties (or abilities, or powers) of the soul. A third faculty (which Plato identified as spiritedness or aggression) is the power that rouses us to fight or to assert ourselves in the face of opposition. According to Plato the soul is like a chariot in which reason holds the reins and the two horses are desire (a black horse) and spiritedness (a white horse). The charioteer can rule his emotions by helping one set of emotions keep the other in check. In the *Republic*, Plato relates each of the cardinal virtues to the faculties of the soul. Thus *good sense* is the virtue that governs reason, *courage* harnesses our spiritedness, and *temperateness* tempers our

Platos chariot of reason

desires. *Justice*, according to Plato, is the virtue that governs the relationship between these three virtues and maintains right balance in the soul.

In his great work the *Summa Theologiae*, Thomas Aquinas took up Plato's idea that the cardinal virtues relate to the faculties of the soul, but he changed this picture slightly because he was able to draw on the idea that human beings possess a 'will' or rational appetite. The idea of the human will was an insight developed by Augustine and not available to Plato or Aristotle. Aquinas therefore relates the four cardinal virtues to four faculties. Two of these belong to our emotional nature: desire, which needs to be informed by *temperateness*; and spiritedness or aggression, which needs to be informed by *courage*. Two belong to our rational nature: practical reason, which needs to be informed by *good sense*; and the will or rational appetite which needs to be informed by *justice*. Thomas Aquinas also agreed with Plato and Aristotle that these four virtues, while they can be distinguished, nevertheless constitute a unity, which is the basis of a well-integrated good character.

Vices, pseudo-virtues & the ambiguity of 'values'

Moral education consists in integral formation of the person through cultivating the virtues. This is best shown by looking in more detail at some particular virtues and considering how they are best acquired. However, before considering the acquisition of virtue it is worth looking at some alternatives to or counterfeits of virtue. In a word, it is worth considering *vice*.

A vice is not simply a lack of virtue, the lack of a fixed disposition to do the right thing. A vice is a settled disposition to do the wrong thing, or to do the right 'external' thing but in the wrong way. If virtue is in some ways like a skill, for example the skill of being able to play the piano, vice is not simply the lack of a skill through inexperience; it is like someone who exercises a skill badly, for example because of accumulated bad habits. Vice is like the tendency of someone who has been taught badly (or who has taught himself badly) to make the same mistakes while playing, and perhaps not even to recognise them as mistakes. He has come to like playing in this way (over-emotionally, or too loud, or too fast). It is his way. However, this disposition to play in his own way may prevent him entering into the tradition of classical music (or Jazz, or any particular genre) because he 'cannot' unlearn his own idiosyncrasies. Entrenched habits are notoriously difficult to break and any teacher would prefer a student who was untutored to a student who had already developed bad habits.

> A vice is a settled disposition to do the wrong thing, or to do the right 'external' thing but in the wrong way.

Vices, like virtues, are built up by practice and past decisions. The beginning of vice is a process of corruption, so that doing the wrong thing becomes easier and more part of a 'second nature'. For example, someone joining a criminal gang may first keep look out when some act of violence is done, or may be asked to hide illegal property or cooperate in some other small ways. He is (mis-)educated to dull his conscience and gradually made comfortable with what is happening until the time comes when

he pulls the trigger himself. This is a threshold moment, after which there is no going back (or no easy going back: in fact repentance is always possible, but it becomes more costly). By the time of his first kill the young villain is already well practised in making excuses to himself. It is but one more step. Such a process is very astutely described in the case of Michael Corleone, the central character of Mario Puzo's novel *The Godfather*. Vices, then, are the product of the wrong kind of education, and the wrong kind of education is much worse than no education at all.

Vices, typically, lie at the extremes. One of Aristotle's great insights was to realise that virtue is a mean between extremes, not a simple arithmetical average but a disposition to act, 'at the right times, with reference to the right objects, towards the right people, with the right motive, and in the right way'. For every virtue, he thought, there are at least two vices, a vice of erring by doing too much and a vice of erring by doing too little.

If we do not realise that virtue is a mean between two vices then it is easy to mistake a vice for a virtue. For example, if we thought that courage were simply the opposite of cowardice, then we might believe that a love of danger was somehow a virtue. However, danger-seeking for its own sake is not a true virtue but a counterfeit, a disguised vice that we might call a pseudo-virtue. Courage lies between the vice of cowardice and the less obvious (but no less real) vice of recklessness. Someone who is reckless shows a failure to take responsibility for his own life and for those who will suffer if he recklessly loses his life. He does not fear enough the loss of what he should hold dear. A reckless person fears too little because he loves too little.

Ethics: Tolerance

Another example of a pseudo-virtue might be the vice of excessive tolerance. True tolerance is the virtue of respecting the freedom of others to be themselves within the context of a shared understanding of the common good. It is a mean between restrictive intolerance (not enough tolerance) and negligent permissiveness (too much tolerance or tolerance in the wrong way or in the wrong circumstances). If we only think of tolerance as the opposite of intolerance or bigotry then we might forget that more tolerance will not always be a good thing. Should racist views be tolerated? What about bullying or intimidation, or teachers expressing opinions in class such as that 'girls do not make good scientists'? We should be surprised if any school claimed a commitment to 'intolerance', yet most schools proudly adopt an explicit policy of 'zero-tolerance' towards at least some repellent views and behaviours. (Of course, schools must also guard against fashionable forms of intolerance: it is wrong to punish the non-threatening expression of certain opinions, whether these are true or false.) It is quite imaginable that a school may err by tolerating some behaviour that requires corrective action, while at the same time err by punishing other forms of behaviour that should be tolerated. Being consistent in this virtue will require not only a kind of assertiveness related to *courage* but also careful judgement informed by the virtue of *good sense*.

It has become common for schools to express their aims by references to various 'statements of values' that they wish to promote. However, the example of tolerance shows why discussion of 'values' can sometimes be ambiguous or misleading. The virtue of tolerance is a good thing, and in this sense a value, but to *understand* tolerance is to see that it integrates different valuable goods: not only the good of allowing freedom to others, but also and at the same time, the solidarity with others and safeguarding of others that puts limits on what it is virtuous to tolerate. If we think of tolerance only as a 'value' we may be misled into believing that more is always better. On the other hand, if we recognise tolerance as a virtue we will expect to find vices on both sides. Similarly, it is good to encourage in students an ethic of hard work without which it is unlikely they will achieve academic success or find fulfilling employment. However, a work ethic or self-discipline is also a virtue that lies between laziness, on the one hand, and on the other an inability to relax, let go, or attend to other goods such as friendship and family life. All work and no play makes Jack a workaholic.

> True tolerance is the virtue of respecting the freedom of others to be themselves within the context of a shared understanding of the common good.

In *Christ at the Centre*, Mgr Stock lists sixteen 'Gospel values': 'Faithfulness and integrity; dignity and compassion; humility and gentleness; truth and justice; forgiveness and mercy; purity and holiness; tolerance and peace; service and sacrifice' (A5.1). Most of these values refer to a virtue possessed by a good person (for example, mercy) though some are names of actions or expressions of virtue (for example, service). What might be the consequence of understanding these values as virtues? We have already seen one example in relation to tolerance: how might these values relate to virtues such as humility or purity? The virtue of justice is one of the cardinal virtues and is explored below.

This reflection shows that, rather than speaking in a vague way of 'values' that we support, we need to identify whether these named values are best understood as virtues and, if so, where virtue lies. What are the various goods that need to be integrated by the virtues? How can we identify what is good, reasonable, right and just in particular cases? The virtues need to be integrated in the life of each person, thus education should seek the *integral formation of the person*, the simultaneous formation of the different aspects of a good character (the virtues) so that they comprise a well-integrated unity.

Good sense and conscience

When it comes to morality, modern society has various contradictory thoughts. On the one hand people strongly believe that some things are utterly wrong (like racism, terrorism, child abuse, and most if not all criminal behaviour). At the same time many people believe, or say they believe, that there is no such thing as 'objective' right and wrong. What is right for one person may be wrong for another. Sometimes they combine these two views to create a third which is internally contradictory; for example when someone argues that, because right and wrong are subjective, it is therefore wrong to 'impose your view of right and wrong' on others. However, we

Section 1

cannot coherently assert that it is always wrong for someone to impose his morality on others. For by so doing we would be imposing our morality on him. More generally, if there were no objective right and wrong then intolerance could not be 'wrong' objectively but only 'wrong for me'. If we wish to speak of 'right' and 'wrong', of 'ought' and 'should', of 'harm' and 'injustice' and avoid contradicting ourselves, it seems we must accept these as objective aspects of the human world. Moral beliefs, for example about what is a fair way to share out a cake, can be true or false: they can be mistaken and they can be corrected.

> Moral beliefs, for example about what is a fair way to share out a cake, can be true or false.

As we have seen, Aristotle says that virtue is a mean between extremes, but not an arithmetic average; rather, it is a disposition to act 'at the right times, with reference to the right objects, towards the right people, with the right motive, and in the right way'. This may be difficult to assess, but the fact that it is sometimes difficult to determine what we should do does not mean that 'there are no right and wrong answers'. In general, in practical matters there are a number of wrong answers and at least one (often more) morally possible answers to the question what we ought to do.

After we have ruled out some possibilities as unjust (or inherently contrary to some other virtue) or as ineffective (or impractical for some other reason) we will typically still be left with more than one way to solve a practical problem, and different solutions will have different advantages and disadvantages. Political decisions, such as whether to build a new railway line between the North and South of England or where to build a new airport, will often require careful balancing of different interests and part of fairness will be the process of making a decision. This should involve open consultation and opportunities to look at alternative suggestions. However, consultation cannot go on forever and eventually a decision must be made. Good sense is the virtue that informs our practical decisions, when they are made well. It helps us to integrate diverse human goods and to apply moral principles in particular situations. There are different areas of decision making (government, domestic decisions, business, sport etc.) and in each area there will be a need for wise decisions and an appropriate form of good sense.

> Good sense is the virtue that informs our practical decisions, when they are made well.

Just as there are pseudo-virtues in relation to courage (danger-seeking) and tolerance (excessive permissiveness) so there are also pseudo-virtues that appear to be forms of good sense but in fact are vices. Good sense seeks genuine reasons for practical decisions, but it can happen that someone does not genuinely want to find a practical way to do the good or right thing. Someone may wish instead to avoid doing what he or she recognises to be good, because it would require courage or because some other option is more immediately desirable. In these circumstances people look for plausible-sounding reasons to rationalise their decision. When this happens at the level of government, politicians turn to the misuse of rhetoric, and to the selective use or manipulation of evidence, in order to provide official 'reasons' for a decision. This political vice, which in modern times is called 'spin', has an equivalent at an individual level. It is called 'rationalisation'. The danger with acquiring the tendency to 'rationalise' our actions is that we may start believing our own excuses. This prevents us acquiring the genuine virtue of good sense.

Another vice that is sometimes confused with good sense is a form of practical reasoning that is willing to embrace injustice, or other evils, for the sake of some strongly desirable good. This vice may be called 'crude pragmatism'. It is distinct from 'rationalisation' in that it is genuinely directed towards actions (and not towards making excuses after the fact) and in that someone who is crudely pragmatic in this sense may be quite open about his or her practical reasoning. However, crude pragmatism is a vice and this is generally easier to see if we consider the more extreme cases. In warfare or in business, the temptation of crude pragmatism is that it makes more options available, and makes it easier to oppose enemies or competitors. However, there is widespread acknowledgment that there is something very objectionable about the means employed by terrorists and by organised criminals (for example targeting civilians and the use of threats of violence in business negotiation) and not only something wrong with their goals. If such criminal practices are morally unacceptable, then it is simply not the case that 'all is fair in love and war'. In general crude pragmatism fails to recognise the unity of the virtues. Good sense is the virtue that helps us find practical means to our ends, but for this to be a *virtue* it must be integrated with other virtues and find good means to good ends. It is possible for a burglar to excel in the skills of his chosen occupation, and he might have enough good sense not to get caught, but this is not a virtue and he will not be flourishing overall, because he does not act in accordance with the virtue of justice.

Practical reasoning informed by good sense is essentially concerned with the question: 'what should I do?' It is thus about making decisions for myself or, to put it another way, about taking responsibility for my own actions. Hence it is about me. This is what people sometimes mean when they talk about 'conscience'. Our conscience is our capacity to make considered judgements recognising the moral quality of an action. We should never go against our conscience because we should seek always to do what is good (this is what we mean by 'should' in a moral sense). We should not be bullied or be distracted or otherwise led to act in a way we think to be wrong. Conscience can rightly be described as that personal core and sanctuary where an individual stands before God. However, this is not because conscience is infallible (it is not), or because we always know ourselves better than others know us (we may not), or because moral judgments are inaccessible to reason or argument (they are not). It is simply that eventually we must act and take responsibility for our actions and do the best we can. No one can do this for us.

> Our conscience is our capacity to make considered judgements recognising the moral quality of an action.

Unfortunately, even if we follow our conscience we may get it wrong, and other people may suffer as a result. To avoid doing harm by accident each of us therefore needs to inform our consciences, for example, by consulting and reflecting on the teaching and example of people we respect, and by practising the virtue of good sense. Only in this way can we discern and thence do what is right and just.

Ethics: Informed Conscience

In relation to the Christian tradition, the thought that we always ought to follow the dictates of conscience might seem to lend support to the idea that where there is moral disagreement, the Church should take a back seat in favour of 'personal conscience'. However, to think in this way is to risk 'wallowing in the luxury of a merely individualistic morality' Vatican II, *The Church in the Modern World* (1965), §30. The idea of an *informed conscience* is the way to understand the proper relation between the moral authority of the Church and the duty to exercise the virtue of good sense. Hand in hand with our obligation to follow our conscience is the need and responsibility to form our conscience according to the truth. In this way, conscience is distinguished from personal preference, or an arbitrary private intuition, and is an important part of the integral formation of the person.

'...The education of conscience is indispensable for human beings who are subjected to negative influences and   tempted by sin to prefer their own judgment and to reject authoritative teachings. The education of the conscience is a lifelong task. From the earliest years, it awakens the child to the knowledge and practice of the interior law recognized by conscience. Prudent education teaches virtue; it prevents or cures fear, selfishness and pride, resentment arising from guilt, and feelings of complacency, born of human weakness and faults. The education of the conscience guarantees freedom and engenders peace of heart.' *Catechism of the Catholic Church* paragraphs 1783-1784.

Justice

Justice is the disposition of our will (our rational appetite) which inclines us to give each person his or her due. We are used to thinking of justice as a measure of outcomes or relationships or states of affairs, the justice of this trial or the justice of wealth distribution within that society or between these countries. However, according to the way of thinking developed in this chapter, justice is first and foremost a virtue; that is, a character trait of the just man or woman. Justice inclines us to be fair, to show respect to every person, to give every person what is due. It is secondarily a quality of an outcome or a relationship or a society when judged by the measure of what a just person would do or seek.

Justice is the disposition of our will (our rational appetite) which inclines us to give each person his or her due.

Ethics: Justice as fairness

Justice is intimately connected with 'fairness' which means applying an appropriate measure and applying it equally to all to whom it is appropriate. In a sense this means treating everyone equally, but it does not imply that the concrete outcomes will be the same for all. A common complaint of small children is that teachers are 'unfair'. But what is it for a teacher to be fair? A teacher who treated every pupil in exactly the same way (for example, by awarding every child the same test marks and writing identical termly reports) could hardly be said to be acting fairly. It is first necessary to determine what is being measured and why before we can determine what it would be to apply the measure equally and hence fairly. An exam might be unfair because it was not testing fairly what it purported to test, for example if a mathematics exam presupposed general knowledge not provided in the question or in the curriculum in relation to the money used in Britain prior to decimalisation. This would put some candidates from some backgrounds at an unfair advantage. On the other hand, there might be no unfairness about the same questions if the topic was explicitly part of the curriculum, for example as part of the history syllabus.

Since justice, according to Aristotle, is the giving of what is owed or fitting to the recipient, it is important to know two things: 1) what is the purpose or nature of the thing or benefit being 'distributed,' and 2) what qualities or talents are we honouring or respecting which qualify the recipient to receive the benefit. This can be seen in the disqualification of a winning athlete who tests positive for performance enhancing drugs. We need to be clear about what a particular athletic event is (say, to run 100 metres in the shortest time), but also what human qualities we honour when we celebrate athletic champions. The drug-taking athlete is not exhibiting the qualities we honour in champions (sportsmanship, natural athletic excellence, etc.) but only pretending to. So the 100 metres is clearly about more than simply completing the distance in the shortest possible time. The person who takes drugs is 'cheating' because he or she breaks the rules of the game and puts himself or herself at an unfair advantage. However there is more to it than this: the cheat claims the honour of a champion but is not performing in the way that a champion would perform, as someone whose victory can be ascribed principally to his or her spirit, endurance, and natural ability.

Justice concerns relationships between persons (or between persons and the community or between the community and persons) in respect to certain goods. However, it is important to realise that justice is not only about goods which have to be shared out because they are finite and divisible. There are also human goods which can be held in common and which may be enjoyed by a large number of people simultaneously, and in their entirety. A good example would be the philosophical discussion that accompanies the drinking of wine. Every mouthful of wine enjoyed by Liz is a mouthful of wine that cannot be enjoyed by Margaret. If Liz drinks more of the wine, then there is less to be enjoyed by Margaret. However, the discussion about ethics that the two women carry on while sharing the wine is a common good. It remains undivided and can be enjoyed in its entirety by both. It may be that Liz derives intense pleasure from the conversation, but this does not mean that Margaret has to enjoy the conversation to a lesser degree. If John joins them, the wine will be further divided, but the conversation may be equally pleasurable. It may even become more stimulating as a result of having a third person join in.

A common good is something more than the sum of lots of individual goods.

In general, a common good is something more than the sum of lots of individual goods. There are many kinds of common goods as there are many forms of shared human activity: from enjoying a meal to building a cathedral, from running businesses to organising concerts or sports events. The education of children depends on many such communal activities, not least in sustaining the life of a school. Finally, there is a common good that comprises the shared good of society as a whole, ordered by justice, and this is sometimes termed the Common Good (with the definite article and/or with capital letters). The common good of a school is both ordered towards, and is a constitutive element of, the Common Good.

As individual citizens may or may not act justly towards other citizens and towards the Common Good, there is also the justice owed by the community to an individual (a justice that is another important element of the Common Good). This is what we call *distributive* justice. Distributive justice has to take into account the different needs and merits of different people. Even in the most egalitarian societies there is an understanding that some people are more worthy of honour in relation to that society, and certainly people have different needs from one another. Justice, remember, does not mean treating people identically; it consists in giving people what they deserve or what is owing to them. From a Christian perspective there is more to say about justice, but not less. Justice inclines us to give to each at *least* what he or she is due.

Distributive justice has to take into account the different needs and merits of different people.

But what does a community owe to *all* of its members? Thomas Aquinas points out that a society exists for the sake of the good life of all its citizens. Society is simply that civic friendship within which individual human beings flourish, taking 'friendship' in a broad sense. Thus it follows that there are certain kinds of behaviour towards its citizens that a society (in this context we might say a state) cannot engage in if it is to have any claim to be a just society. We might explain this by analogy with the activity of a doctor. If a patient complains of a headache, the doctor might have to explore all kinds of possible diagnoses and treatments in order to treat the headache. If the cause of the headache was found to be a brain tumour, say, then the treatment might be painful and arduous. What is certain is that cutting the patient's head off would not be an option, for while this would certainly arrest the headache, it could not be regarded as 'treatment'. Just as a doctor could not prescribe decapitation as a treatment for a headache, a society could not set out to harm its harmless citizens. A society which set out to harm or kill its citizens as such would be a counterfeit and unjust society.

Elizabeth Anscombe

For this reason Elizabeth Anscombe states that, while there are examples where it is difficult to say what justice requires, someone who is just (who possesses the virtue of justice) will at least recognise that the deliberate killing of the innocent is an injustice. In fact, there is no point reasoning with anyone who is not just in at least this minimal sense. Hence Anscombe says quite bluntly that 'if someone really thinks, in advance, that it is an open question whether such an action as procuring the judicial execution of the innocent should be quite excluded from consideration – I do not want to argue with him; he shows a corrupt mind' (*Human Life, Action and Ethics*, page 191).

Courage & temperateness

Courage is the disposition that enables us to act well in the face of what is arduous or dangerous. There is nothing wrong with the emotion of fear in itself, of course. Some phobias, such as genuphobia (fear of knees), pogonophobia (fear of beards) and arachibutyrophobia (fear of peanut butter sticking to the roof of one's mouth), are genuinely irrational. However, others such as mysophobia (fear of germs), and selachophobia (fear of sharks), are rational in kind if not in every situation where the fear may arise. The point is that 'the right thing to do' is often difficult or dangerous, even frightening, and courage is what allows us to face that difficulty. As stated earlier, courage is a mean between the extremes of cowardice and recklessness.

Courage is a virtue which should be in evidence in the field of education. While we might hope that school would not be a cause of mortal fear, learning can be arduous. The business of gaining knowledge and understanding, and the business of acquiring virtuous dispositions, is not always easy. It can often require courage in the broad sense of strength of character to tell the truth or do the right thing, and also to complete difficult tasks such as learning times-tables or the subjunctive in a foreign language. In general, courage is the virtue that leads us to aspire to greatness and excellence and not limit ourselves to the safe path in order to avoid disappointment.

> Courage is the disposition that enables us to act well in the face of what is arduous or dangerous.

Selachophobia (fear of sharks, is a rational reaction).

Many people, though they would regard themselves as 'successful', have settled for a small existence which includes, but does not go beyond, for example, an artfully decorated home, a fast car, and sometimes a carefree life without commitments which deliberately excludes deep and lasting relationships and children. Indeed, marriage

Section 1

and children are probably the two areas which most demand the exercise of courage in the lives of most men and women. This particular aspect of the virtue of courage is called magnanimity, or great-heartedness. It is the magnanimous person who is spurred to excellence, to do something great or worthwhile with his or her life.

Another flavour of the virtue of courage which is worth mentioning, because it is not mentioned very often, is what Thomas Aquinas called magnificence. This is a virtue which certainly ought to be possessed by teachers and all those charged with something as important as the education of children. Magnificence is the virtue needed to complete big projects requiring substantial expenditure (financial and human). A glance at pettiness, the vice most directly opposed to it, helps to show what magnificence is about. The petty person is concerned to keep expenditure down – not a bad thing in itself – but allows that concern to unsettle the balance there ought to be between the cost of something and the value of doing it. The magnificent person, on the other hand, looks to the greatness of the work being undertaken, its value, and not simply to the cost. Of course, he or she is not indifferent to the cost but does not allow fear of the cost to prevent great works being done where this is possible and reasonable.

There is another vice opposed to magnificence: the vice of waste, where the balance between the value of something and its cost is tipped in the other direction – we don't pay sufficient attention to the cost of something in relation to its value. Waste in this sense is generally unsustainable so that the resources needed for a task, including, one might add, the human resources, are burned up or burned out. Concern with protecting one's time and space can be a kind of pettiness, but some reasonable care of the self (some 'counting of the cost') is clearly needed to sustain a project of education which is accomplished only over years.

Whereas courage helps us face dangers and arduous tasks, temperateness is the disposition that enables us act and react well in the face of what is desirable. It is usually translated in English as 'temperance', but here we shall use 'temperateness' in order to make a point. Just as the word 'courage' makes us think of soldiers and explorers, 'temperance' makes us think about teetotallers. We also think of temperance as involving an effort of will and demanding self-control. However, this is not what a virtue necessarily involves; on the contrary, a virtue, when it has been perfectly acquired, becomes 'second nature'. The temperate person does not have to restrain herself through an effort of will, but acts easily and naturally.

> Temperateness is the disposition that enables us to act and react well in the face of what is desirable.

The principal areas in which we need to show the virtue of temperateness are those most closely linked to our 'sensual appetites': eating, drinking, and sex. A vice obviously contrary to temperateness is gluttony, but the person who apparently subsists upon lettuce leaves cannot be said to be temperate either. Temperateness is like Goldilocks' porridge – neither too hot nor too cold, but just right. Temperateness in eating and drinking clearly involves taking what is necessary for our life and health, but there is another important aspect to eating and drinking. Food and drink create and strengthen friendship, so the temperate person also has an eye to what is necessary to the enjoyment of his friends. A single glass of champagne may be nutritionally insignificant in itself, but when drunk to toast a newly married couple it is far from insignificant. The person who refuses the wedding champagne because the latest detox diet regime is more important is displaying a kind of self-indulgence not so far removed from that of the glutton.

The kind of desire that finds expression in romantic love is, by its very character, one that seeks out a relationship with another person that is mutual and unconditional.

In relation to sexual desires it is clear that we all, whatever our particular state of life, need to integrate this side of our emotional life with the rest of our personality. The form of temperateness that tempers our sexual desires is called chastity. It is not only practical considerations that justify the link between chaste love, sexual desire, and marriage. The kind of desire that finds expression in romantic love is, by its very character, one that seeks out a relationship with another person that is mutual and unconditional. Sex without this kind of commitment is something less than fully human, a kind of using rather than a kind of loving (or at least, a loving that is seriously defective). People talk of 'making love', but if there is no unconditional commitment this may be somewhat of a euphemism. It is also evident that a relationship of unconditional, public commitment is the best environment within which to bring up a child, where he or she can have a positive relationship with both parents and experience a stable emotional environment.

Often ethics teaching in regard to sex is reduced to obtaining consent and using contraception. However, different forms of contraception raise their own ethical questions. For example, standard forms of the contraceptive pill and other hormonal contraceptives sometimes act by preventing an embryonic human being from implanting in the womb, and other forms undermine the important link between sex, self giving love and marriage. More broadly, even where contraception is used, sexual intercourse typically retains the possibility, and hence the responsibility, of the couple conceiving a child. If this possibility is not acknowledged then, when a child is conceived, he or she may not be acknowledged, and may be killed quietly by abortion before he or she is born. This is not a necessary consequence of unchastity, for a couple may be unchaste but still welcome the child of their misplaced love, but here it will require the virtue of courage to rescue a failure of temperateness. Catholic teaching on these topics is clear, if controversial and hard to articulate in our secular culture. A profound personal and theological approach relating to the full human meaning of, and the responsibility we have for, our bodily actions is explored for example in John Paul II's *Theology of the Body*.

Section 1

Ethics: Respect in relationships

Chastity does not simply mean not having sex. It means only having sex where and when and how and with whom this would be appropriate, as well as recognising the fundamental link between sex and fertility. It involves thinking and acting appropriately with friends and colleagues, and what thoughts we indulge or cultivate (for all good and bad actions begin in the imagination), and within a marital relationship, it means being honest and sensitive without selfishness or thoughtlessness hindering the communication of love. Those who teach 'natural family planning', which involves abstaining from sex at fertile times of the woman's cycle, sometimes hear that couples have found this to be a positive experience precisely because it requires them to communicate and to respect one another. Nevertheless, no technique, however good in itself, is a substitute for respect if this is not already present in a relationship.

The need for temperateness is evident not only in relation to desire for food and sexual pleasure, but in relation to desire for wealth, for honour, for attention, for entertainment, for challenge, for adventure; in short, to all of our desires. All human desires, however worthy in themselves, can become damaging obsessions. On the other hand, insufficient desire for good things can make us cold, dull and lifeless. Even in relation to knowledge or wisdom, the fulfilment of the mind, there can be an excess, a curiosity that prevents us seeing the wood for the trees, as well as the lack of desire shown by boredom or indifference. This brings us to the subject of the vices and virtues of learning and of teaching – that is, to education, which is the specific topic of the next chapter.

3. Education & Ethos

Some pointers for making use of this chapter

This chapter provides a definition of a 'school' and a definition of 'ethos'. Both of these may be useful topics for INSET days, but these topics are also reminders of the essential need for good induction of new staff in order for the practice proclaimed by the community to be a reality. For, as this chapter makes clear, the actual ethos of a school will be constituted not by fine sounding mission statements but by 'the beliefs and behaviour of staff and students, and these will be shaped not only by school itself but also by pressures and presuppositions of wider society'.

The discussion of sex and relationships education in this chapter again implies the need for good induction – in order for new teachers to be presented with the Catholic viewpoint on sexual ethics, together with the aims of education and the dignity of the human person. It is a challenge for any school to ensure that the diverse occurrences of references to sex across different disciplines (Sex and Relations Education [where this exists as a subject], Geography, Biology, and Religious Education [statutory and examined]) and in the pastoral practice of the school, express a common understanding. Induction is the opportunity to build a common understanding across the school which can then be refreshed and augmented by in-service training. The present chapter provides some essential materials for this.

Curriculum Links

OCR

G571: AS Philosophy of Religion (Ancient Greek influences)

AQA RS

AS Unit H (Religion in Contemporary Society)

AQA Philosophy

Unit 3 PHIL3 Key Themes in Philosophy (Epistemology and Metaphysics)

Unit 4 PHIL4 Philosophical Problems (Plato)

Edexcel

Religious Studies Units 1-4 (Faith in Schools)

The primacy of learning over teaching

Learning can happen without teaching (as for example when learning occurs through 'trial and error' or by self-directed reading) but teaching cannot happen without learning. If no learning occurs then no teaching has occurred (only an attempt at teaching). To put it another way, teaching is for the sake of learning, not learning for the sake of teaching. A teacher may find his or her work fulfilling, at least on a good day, but the aim of teaching is not directed towards fulfilling the teacher but towards supporting the learner. A good teacher will be one who finds fulfilment precisely in supporting the learning of the learner.

It is common for our parents or older siblings to have a treasury of stories concerning the cute things that we said and did as a child. These tales are frequently wheeled out at family occasions and sometimes embarrass us in front of friends or colleagues. The family of Thomas Aquinas preserved one such story about his childhood. Thomas came from a wealthy and well-connected family and the infant theologian, we are told, liked to ask guests coming to the family home, 'What is God?' It seems that he never received a satisfactory answer to this deceptively simple question because he devoted the rest of his life to trying to answer it. Even then, he finally decided that it was a question that he could not satisfactorily answer.

Children, especially young children, are adept at asking very simple questions which are nonetheless extremely difficult to answer. The natural desire of the child to ask questions is good news for those involved in education. We assume that the child does not ask questions to be difficult (though from time to time this undoubtedly happens), but out of a desire to know and understand. This fact was noted by Aristotle at the beginning of his *Metaphysics* when he observed, 'All men by nature desire to know.'

'All men by nature desire to know. An indication of this is the delight we take in our senses; for even apart from their usefulness they are loved for themselves; and above all others the sense of sight. For not only with a view to action, but even when we are not going to do anything, we prefer seeing (one might say) to everything else. The reason is that this, most of all the senses, makes us know and brings to light many differences between things.' Aristotle *Metaphysics*

There is an important difference between Aristotle's view of knowledge and that of Plato, his teacher. Plato believed that all learning is only a process of remembering. He thought that before we were born we had direct knowledge of the true and perfect forms of things and that this knowledge is still innate in us. When we see some geometrical shape in nature, or hear the harmony of a tune for the first time, or follow the logic of an argument, what we are doing, according to Plato, is recognising in things those forms that we once knew. Plato thought that the actual world we see is only a shadow of the perfect world we once saw and now dimly remember.

Plato (L) & Aristotle (R)

In contrast Aristotle thought that our five senses give us knowledge of the real world and that if we discover something, then this is new knowledge (at least new to us). He considered Plato's forms to be abstractions of real things. Thus if an orange is not perfectly spherical this is not because oranges are defective (not as good as the idea of a perfect sphere); it is because a sphere is not adequate as a description of an orange. The real orange is not an abstract idea but is dimpled, bright, tangible and tangy, and we know about it only through our senses.

'Be ye doers of the word, not hearers only, deceiving yourselves' James 1:22

Unfortunately, Aristotle's claim that 'knowledge comes through the senses' was misunderstood by some later thinkers. John Locke argued that the mind was like a blank slate (a *tabula rasa*), which was filled by sense impressions. This seemed to make knowledge something purely passive, as if we merely received the impressions made on us by the objects around us. A more recent philosopher, Karl Popper, satirised this as the 'bucket theory' of knowledge. The mind is like an empty bucket which fills up as it receives information from the senses. What is missing from the bucket theory is that learning is always an activity. Objects are not passively observed but touched and prodded and explored from different angles. Reflect how babies explore the world around them with all their senses: each and every item is grasped, shaken, pulled apart and thrust into the mouth. Even in maturity, when told that paint is wet or informed that a dinner plate is hot, we want to 'see for ourselves'. Rather than shrinking back we are filled with an intense desire to reach out and touch it, 'Ouch! – yes, it is hot isn't it?'

If Aristotle was correct, as seems to be confirmed not only by reflection and experience but by virtually all contemporary educational theory, then learning is essentially active. This is true not only of practical or empirical subjects such as engineering or biology but also of the most abstract subjects such as mathematics or logic. A well-known book on logic starts with a quotation from the Bible, 'Be ye doers of the word, not hearers only, deceiving yourselves' (James 1:22). In order to 'see' the answer to a problem in logic or mathematics we must do many exercises, solve many problems, *learn by doing*, learn what it is we are looking for and how to look for it.

If, though, learning is prior to teaching, and learning is essentially an activity moved *from within* by a natural desire, what role is left for teachers? Why do we need teachers at all? This question is perhaps easiest to answer if we start with our first teachers, our parents or early carers.

The primacy of parents as teachers

The help we need to learn about the world comes first of all from our parents, or those in the role of our parents: those who care for us as we take our first steps (literally and figuratively). Most importantly, our parents teach us language. Children are not left to their own devices and expected to devise their own language. Parents use words themselves and gradually introduce children to ways of doing things with words. As time goes on, new words can be taught by means of recognised words, and language can be used to explain, qualify, or correct our understanding. However our first words are not 'explained' in this way so much as 'picked up' by living with and depending on those close to us. We start with a shared life and natural inclinations and reactions (including emotional reactions) and these provide the basis for learning a shared linguistic and cultural life.

Parents, to act well as parents, must already possess moral virtues to some degree, and their children learn from them. From infancy parents teach lessons about justice when sharing toys, courage in the face of knocks and bruises, temperateness in the matter of eating sweets, and many other virtues. But parents also have intellectual virtues, that is, those habits that enable us to learn well (about which more below). They begin to train their children too in these from birth.

Children will learn to take an interest in what parents seem to take an interest in

Almost without thinking, parents will encourage their children to pick out objects and to notice similarities or difference between objects of the different colours or shapes. Indeed such training is essential to the acquisition of language – a child who is shown a red plastic brick while an adult says 'red!' cannot know whether 'red' is the name of the thing, its shape, its colour, its weight, its texture or any other feature of it, until he has seen many other 'red' objects. At the same time, parents subtly encourage their children to take an interest in 'more worthy' things. Thus they will point out the big red bus rather than the asphalt of the road; the red robin in the hedgerow and not the discarded plastic bag. Children will learn to take an interest in what parents seem to take an interest in. Such 'directing of attention' is a key to learning.

By the time a child enters 'education' she has in fact been in education for years, with, on average, a 2000-word vocabulary to prove it. Though young children are not yet able to make decisions independently they already express many of the characteristic features that are unique to human beings among all animals. As argued above, every child is a human person in virtue of the nature that all human beings share, irrespective of what powers they currently express. Nevertheless, it is worth noting just how much is typically already expressed by the age of two or three years old. The education that occurs in school presupposes the education that has already occurred, and if for some reason the child has been deprived of the presence of any parent-figure in her early years then it is extremely difficult to remedy this lack. Neglect at the earliest stages of development will show itself not only in learning difficulties but, even more so, in relation to the child's emotional life. This in turn may have an impact on the child's moral and religious development.

Education: The meaning of *'In loco parentis'*

The role of parents as the first educators of their children gives them a duty and hence a right to determine the kind of education that their children receive. The role of teachers is to assist parents in the education of their children and, when the children are at school, teachers have a duty of care which is sometimes described as their acting *in loco parentis*. The parents entrust their child to the school and if, for example, the child is injured during the school day, the parents will rightly demand to know what happened and who had responsibility for the child. This has become an issue in relation to school trips. In another way all teaching in school is in some sense *in loco parentis*, for education as such belongs more properly to parents than to school teachers. The ability of the school to act *in loco parentis* is thus secondary and limited in scope. The school cannot take over the role of the parents completely.

The duty and thus the natural right of parents to oversee the education of their children is somewhat obscured in the United Kingdom, and in other Western countries, by the involvement of the state in education. It is reasonable for the state to make provision for education, especially where parents would otherwise lack the means to provide a good level of education for their children. It is also reasonable for the state to act to uphold standards in education (for example in relation to public examinations) and to set the curricula to be covered in state-funded schools. However, except where a child's safety is at risk, the state acts unjustly if it takes from parents their responsibility for the child's education. This has implications for the idea of parental choice in education: the choice of school, whether secular or religious, single-sex or co-educational, state, voluntary aided or independent, or the choice to home-educate, as well as the choice to withdraw children from certain lessons or activities (such as sex education or religious services). Parental choice of how to provide for their child's education is not a privilege to be sought from the state. It is a right essential to parenthood and more fundamental than the state itself.

Schooling & ethos

Learning is an activity of the learner, and inasmuch as it is supported by education, this is primarily the achievement of the parents or those who are acting as parents. What then is the role of schools and school teachers? Schools are places of learning established to assist parents in the education of their children by providing access to specialised knowledge and skills and to the cultural legacy of previous generations. They also provide a context to learn social virtues, so that, by learning together, pupils also learn to be together. This last aspect is not to be underestimated. However the first purpose of schooling, and what school teachers provide that cannot, at least in general, be provided by parents on their own, is the systematic and disciplined cultivation of the mind. Parents can feed the curiosity of children and encourage in them a love of reading and a desire for knowledge, but few parents have the skills to be able to take children through a full range of subjects systematically. Schools thus provide where parents cannot. Nevertheless, parental influence and parental responsibility remain.

In the collaboration of parents and schools, perhaps no areas of education are so sensitive as *sex and relationships education*, sometimes included in *personal, social, health and economic education*. This area of education has never been easy but it is made more problematic by a pervasive culture of distrust of parents. Among healthcare professionals, in particular, there seems to be an expectation that teenagers will be sexually active and a tendency to frame 'sexual health' as a technical question of reducing the risk of pregnancy and of sexually transmitted infection. In this frame, parents feature only as a possible or actual obstacle to the planned 'harm reduction'. This problematic culture is generally less pronounced in a school context where teachers are more likely to be concerned about the integral human development of the child. Nevertheless, sex and relationships education is an area where it is reasonable for parents to be wary, especially if healthcare professionals or other specialists, including sex and relationships advisers and political activists, are brought in as speakers as part of the programme of education.

Education in relationships and personal responsibility is not simply or primarily acquisition of impersonal knowledge, still less the acquisition of technical knowledge abstracted from the virtues. Rather, it involves the cultivation of healthy and helpful moral dispositions, centrally temperateness, but also courage, justice, and good sense. Even positive teaching about marriage and chastity is unlikely to be effective on its own without adequate self-esteem and aspiration for the future, both of which seem to be needed in order to resist the dangers of peer pressure. Most of this personal formation of character will occur outside formal education and if classroom teaching is also involved this must build on prior formation. On the other hand, issues that relate to sex, relationships and fertility will arise in many areas of the curriculum, not only in Sex and Relationships Education (where this exists as a subject) but in Geography, Biology, Religious Education (statutory and examined) and also in the systems of discipline and pastoral support within the school. It is not an area of education that can be avoided. The challenge, therefore, will be to ensure that these diverse occurrences express a common understanding.

> Schools are places of learning established to assist parents in the education of their children by providing access to specialised knowledge and skills and to the cultural legacy of previous generations. They also provide a context to learn social virtues, so that, by learning together, pupils also learn to be together.

What is true of sex and relationships education is true of education more generally. Moral and intellectual virtues are expressed, practised, and communicated not through a single specialist subject but through many areas of the curriculum simultaneously, as well as through structures and practices of discipline and of pastoral support, and through the general pattern of behaviour of staff and students. These beliefs, attitudes, and practices will be more or less coherent, more or less overt, and by design or default will constitute the character of the school, much as virtues or vices constitute the character of a person. Ethos is the pattern of belief and practice of a community that embodies and expresses its fundamental dispositions

> Ethos is the pattern of belief and practice of a community that embodies and expresses its fundamental dispositions and objectives.

and objectives. Sometimes a school will attempt to encapsulate its ethos in a mission statement or in a motto, but such statements are secondary. They are not the source of the ethos of the school and may or may not reflect the actual ethos. The actual ethos will be constituted by the beliefs and behaviour of staff and students, and these will be shaped not only by school itself but also by pressures and presuppositions of wider society.

One example of a force that could undermine the desired educational ethos of the school is the relentless pressure schools face to achieve measurable results (especially but not only in relation to exam results and especially but not only as these are ranked in league tables). It has been argued repeatedly in these pages that learning is essentially a vital activity of the learner. Few if any teachers would argue that education is best understood by analogy with the means of mass production, or best assessed by reference to 'units of information' to be amassed and then reproduced under predetermined conditions. Few would say that students are best educated when trained to emulate the unthinking conformism of a machine. However, the desire of governments (of both 'left' and 'right') to improve standards in education and the desire of parents and students to gain qualifications as a means to future life-opportunities, encourage precisely these reductive approaches to assessment. Rather than assessment being shaped by the goals of education, educators are constrained to teach to the assessment. If teachers resist this, they must struggle with 'serving two masters', the external criteria first and, where time allows, the inherent goals of knowledge and understanding. Perhaps this simple dichotomy is a caricature but the challenges that assessment practices pose for ethos are real.

As the means, regularity and forms of assessment express and shape the ethos of a school, so does the content of the curriculum. Just as parents overtly or covertly communicate to children what is worthy of attention so the curriculum of the school implies a judgement about what is worth learning and about whether and how subjects interrelate. Choices must be made, for the potential number of topics is infinite and there is an infinite number of ways in which topics can be ordered or related to one another. The danger is that such choices may express a narrow and fragmented understanding of the human person and of the intellectual tradition. A further danger is that such decisions are taken out of the hands of teachers or schools and are determined at a national level on a political basis. It is not only that decisions made at this level and in this way tend to be made badly, but also that by limiting the scope for schools to shape the curriculum, schools are deprived of the ability to shape their own character. The task of shaping the curriculum is also one that, of necessity, is interdisciplinary, and the effort to do this across the school offers a rare opportunity for teachers to articulate the fundamental aims of the school and the role of each discipline within it.

Section 1

The virtues of learning

Progress in knowledge of a subject will require us to think, consider, compare, read, judge, interpret, search, reflect, evaluate, and other verbs familiar from Bloom's taxonomy. We tend to see these abilities as skills, but it would be better to understand them as intellectual virtues because they are essential elements of a well-formed mind, characteristics of anyone who is able to think and act in an intellectually appropriate and rational way. The intellectual virtues are those dispositions of the mind that enable a person to reason well and to come to a knowledge of the truth. In addition to the moral virtues, Aristotle thus identified five 'intellectual virtues', excellences of the mind, which play a role in human knowing: scientific knowledge, technical ability, practical good sense, wisdom, and intuitive reason.

> The intellectual virtues are those dispositions of the mind that enable a person to reason well and to come to a knowledge of the truth.

Someone who is a novice in some area of scientific knowledge will generally be guided by the conclusions of others, themselves reliant on the work of previous scholars or scientists. Such conclusions are often set out in text books which typically give a rather idealised picture of the process of discovery and the current state of knowledge. The danger for a student is that such books might be regarded as providing 'the answers', as though human authority set down in writing were the strongest form of argument, whereas in fact it is the weakest. This is even more evident when the student leaves the recommended text books and relies on popular articles in newspapers or magazines, or on the internet, which contains much that is of great value but more that is of dubious value or of none at all. It is an important step when a student comes to realise, if he or she does realise, that what is written in the books cannot itself be based on other books and these on other books… *ad infinitum*. Rather the basis of knowledge is human activity: critical engagement with the world, careful and repeated experiments, sensitive observation, returning to the sources, and the dialectic of furious arguments some of which have continued for decades and some of which continue still.

'no man may hope to be a philosopher who has a good memory'
Fr Vincent McNabb

Along with the mistake that books are there to provide the answers is the confusion of thinking with memory. While it is true that a working mind requires memory, in the longer term it is more important to know how to find something out than to remember it, for we cannot remember everything (only God can hold everything in mind at the same time). Furthermore, focus on memorising can distract us from the more important task of thinking, and filling the passive intellect can take the place of exercising the intellectual virtues, hence the paradoxical remark of Fr Vincent McNabb that 'no man may hope to be a philosopher who has a good memory' (*Where Believers May Doubt*, preface).

It may be objected that, in many fields, it is important to have knowledge immediately to hand in order to apply it. Learning by heart is unhelpful if it is a substitute for thinking, but it is helpful if it provides material to reflect on, 'grist to the mill'. As analysing presupposes knowing (and hence memory), so education generally involves an ordered sequence of steps, each building on what has gone before. This is in part a logical requirement of the subject matter (this idea presupposes that idea, this skill depends on the ability to do that) and in part a psychological feature of cognitive development. The mind of a child develops by stages and this should be reflected in the way a subject is taught to a particular age-group. During the twentieth century there have been numerous attempts to specify the stages of this development, perhaps most notably Jean Piaget's theory of cognitive development, Benjamin Bloom's taxonomy of educational objectives, and Lawrence Kohlberg's stages of moral development.

Jean Piaget's Theory of Cognitive Development

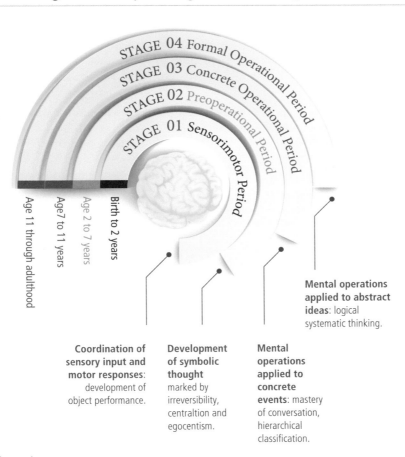

Mental operations applied to abstract ideas: logical systematic thinking.

Coordination of sensory input and motor responses: development of object performance.

Development of symbolic thought marked by irreversibility, centraltion and egocentism.

Mental operations applied to concrete events: mastery of conversation, hierarchical classification.

Age 11 through adulthood

Age7 to 11 years

Age 2 to 7 years

Birth to 2 years

STAGE 04 Formal Operational Period

STAGE 03 Concrete Operational Period

STAGE 02 Preoperational period

STAGE 01 Sensorimotor Period

Diagram 1

Section 1

Benjamin Bloom's Taxonomy of Educational Objectives

Combining information to form a unique product; requires creativity and originality.

EVALUATION

SYNTHESIS

Making decisions and supporting views; requires an understanding of values.

Using information to solve problems; transferring abstract or theoretical ideas to practical situations. Identifying connections and how they apply.

ANALYSIS

APPLICATION

Identifying components; determining arrangement, logic, and semantics.

Memorising verbatum information. Being able to remember, but not understand the material.

COMPREHENSION

KNOWLEDGE

Restating in your own words. paraphrasing, summarising, translating.

Section 1

Diagram 2

Lawrence Kohlberg's Stages of Moral Development

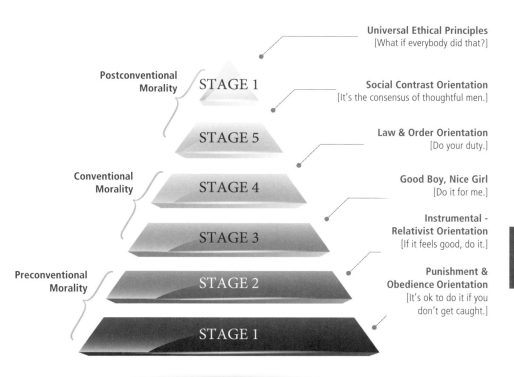

Universal Ethical Principles
[What if everybody did that?]

Postconventional Morality — STAGE 1

Social Contrast Orientation
[It's the consensus of thoughtful men.]

STAGE 5

Law & Order Orientation
[Do your duty.]

Conventional Morality — STAGE 4

Good Boy, Nice Girl
[Do it for me.]

STAGE 3

Instrumental - Relativist Orientation
[If it feels good, do it.]

Preconventional Morality — STAGE 2

Punishment & Obedience Orientation
[It's ok to do it if you don't get caught.]

STAGE 1

Section 1

Diagram 3

In relation to these developmental accounts, it should first be acknowledged that education is most certainly a process of gradual development and that research in developmental psychology has undoubtedly increased our understanding of this process. However, serious thinkers in this area have often been ill-served by disciples or populists, who have taken their carefully-qualified conclusions, simplified and schematised them, and applied them to educational policy. This can easily lead to underestimating the abilities of younger children, for example their aptitude for abstract thought which Piaget wrongly supposed was a capability that emerged only later in development. It might also involve confusion between psychological and philosophical assertions, for example in the claim that belief in moral absolutes represents an 'immature' stage in Kohlberg's model of moral development. This claim begs the question as to whether the most adequate and final moral understanding should or should not include some moral absolutes. A more general problem is that these developmental ideas have been applied within a culture dominated by assessment to specified 'attainment targets'. Such a culture reinforces the tendency to over-specify the developmental process in relation to a number of 'key stages'. Against such tendencies it is a task of teachers to cultivate their own intellectual virtues and to apply to the educational dogmas of the day the right kind of scepticism.

At each stage of development, however we specify them, a child will need motivation to make progress. A good student will cultivate the virtue of studiousness so that she has the stamina needed to do the hard work that study will sometimes require. On the other hand, if the virtue of studiousness is a kind of temperateness that moderates our desire for knowledge, then as well as the vice of lack of desire (laziness, or lack of interest) there will be vices of excess. Thomas Aquinas, who was certainly someone who loved study, warns that there can be a vice of curiosity when the desire to know is disordered and excessive. Curiosity about trivial things can be a distraction that prevents us from reflecting on more important things. Some kinds of curiosity are wrong because they are potentially harmful or hurtful, such as gossip or scandal, or because they encourage prejudice rather than openness to new knowledge. The most vicious form of curiosity is where someone is willing to commit acts of cruelty or injustice in the search for knowledge, or for the power that comes with knowledge.

Ethics: Research ethics

In the ancient world there was a physician called Herophilus (d. 280 BCE) who so wanted to understand the human body that he undertook live dissection of slaves, including pregnant women, to find out how the human body works. His discoveries are important in the history of physiology but he is one of the earliest examples of science pursued without ethical limits. Tertullian (d. 225) said of him 'He hated men that he might know'. During the Second World War the same attitude was shown by some scientists who were willing to experiment on prisoners. They so desired knowledge that they committed crimes against humanity. Nor is our own age immune from this kind of attitude: some secular philosophers have called for severely disabled infants or adults to be used in lethal experiments, and destructive research on human embryos and foetuses is both practised and defended.

Formal education starts with and should feed a love of learning, but even the love of learning needs to be moderated by virtue so that it is directed towards our ultimate goal.

The aims of education

At this point a first attempt can be made to address the question raised in the introduction: What is the point of education? As each kind of living thing has its own characteristic form and flourishes in its own characteristic ways, so there is a characteristic way in which human beings flourish. Human life is not only animal but also 'linguistic', 'cultural', 'political' or 'rational': in a word, human beings are *persons* and find fulfilment in relation to one another, through friendship. The possibility of true friendship, and thus of human flourishing, depends on the integral formation of the person through cultivating the virtues, and it is this that is the aim of education broadly understood. Education is the integral formation of the human person, through the cultivation of the moral and intellectual virtues, for the good of the person and for the common good of society.

> Education is the integral formation of the human person, through the cultivation of the moral and intellectual virtues, for the good of the person and for the common good of society.

> The principal aim of 'liberal education' is 'to exercise the mind neither in art nor in duty' but 'to educate the intellect to reason well in all matters, to reach out towards truth, and to grasp it'.
>
> John Henry Newman, *The Idea of a University*

The first educators of children are parents, or those who take on the role of parents. Schools assist parents in this process of integral formation. However, the contribution of formal education, of schools and school teachers, is more directly concerned with the development of the mind. This can be helpful for moral virtue, for in order to do the right thing it helps if we can think straight. Furthermore, the school, as a moral community, expresses and practises the moral virtues. Nevertheless, in relation to the balance between parental and school education, the school is more directly concerned with the cultivation of the intellectual virtues rather than with the cultivation of the moral virtues, and this relative emphasis will increase as a child progresses from primary to secondary education. In relation to higher education this ideal was expressed well by John Henry Newman (d. 1890) when he argued that the principal aim of what he called a 'liberal education' was 'to exercise the mind neither in art nor in duty' but 'to educate the intellect to reason well in all matters, to reach out towards truth, and to grasp it'. This remark was made in *The Idea of a University* (discourse 6), but it holds at least to some extent also for a school. Schools should teach children to think well.

This is not to deny that education has other overlapping and complementary aims, for every human person inhabits multiple narratives: professional, social, domestic, economic, cultural and so forth. Human activities, especially activities as fundamental as education, will have significance in many spheres. It is undeniable that education is of great importance for the economy and it is reasonable that politicians, businesses, parents and students should be concerned that schools provide a formation that will help young people to find employment within which they can flourish and through which the economic good of society can be promoted. Similarly it is reasonable for governments and communities to wish schools to foster the virtues that make good citizens and that help build up society. Artists and writers may similarly be concerned that schools enable children to develop their creative gifts so that they can appreciate and perhaps contribute to the artistic and cultural life of society. This is sometimes put forward on the basis that 'the arts' contribute to the economy, which is certainly true, but irrespective of its further economic significance, the cultural heritage of society is itself an aspect of the Common Good.

These further aims of education need not and should not be denied, but education is misunderstood if it starts with these other benefits. The danger with starting with the usefulness of education for this or that further purpose is not just that those who identify what is useful (for employment, or for citizenship, or for the promotion of culture etc.) will often have a narrow or unbalanced agenda. More fundamentally, focus on secondary usefulness will always emphasise *particular* skills or aspects of the person and thus characteristically miss the person as a whole. An alternative to this is provided by Jacques Maritain who argued that 'education should essentially aim not at producing a type but at liberating the human person'. Such an emphasis on freedom and on the education of the whole person is also reflected in the teaching of the Catholic Church.

Education: Freedom as the aim of education

'It must never be forgotten that the purpose of instruction at school is education, that is, the development of man from within, freeing him from that conditioning which would prevent him from becoming a fully integrated human being. The school must begin from the principle that its educational programme is intentionally directed to the growth of the whole person.'

'Precisely because the school endeavours to answer the needs of a society characterised by depersonalisation and a mass production mentality which so easily result from scientific and technological developments, it must develop into an authentically formational school, reducing such risks to a minimum. It must develop persons who are responsible and inner-directed, capable of choosing freely in conformity with their conscience. This is simply another way of saying that the school is an institution where young people gradually learn to open themselves up to life as it is, and to create in themselves a definite attitude to life as it should be.' *The Catholic School* Congregation for Catholic Education 1977, paragraphs 29 and 31.

The Church is concerned not only with the idea of a Christian school but with the very idea of a school as such. This has relevance also to Church schools, because 'to understand fully the specific mission of the Catholic school it is essential to keep in mind the basic concept of what a school is; that which does not reproduce the characteristic features of a school cannot be a Catholic school' (*The Catholic School* paragraph 25 emphasis added).

A Christian account of education must therefore include elements that apply to all education and which should, in principle, be accessible to all men and women of good will. Such a universal vision is set out in the Second Vatican Council (1962-1965) which states that all people of every race, condition and age have a right to a true education.

'to understand fully the specific mission of the Catholic school it is essential to keep in mind the basic concept of what a school is; that which does not reproduce the characteristic features of a school cannot be a Catholic school'. *The Catholic School* Congregation for Catholic Education 1977.

Education: The right to education

'All men of every race, condition and age, since they enjoy the dignity of a human being, have an inalienable right to... a true education [which] aims at the formation of the human person in the pursuit of his ultimate end and of the good of the societies of which, as man, he is a member, and in whose obligations, as an adult, he will share.'

'Among all educational instruments the school has a special importance. It is designed not only to develop with special care the intellectual faculties but also to form the ability to judge rightly, to hand on the cultural legacy of previous generations, to foster a sense of values, to prepare for professional life.' Vatican II *Gravissimum Educationis* (paragraphs 1 and 5):

A Catholic account of the aims and virtues of school education will thus include much that can be agreed with non-Catholics. For this reason the virtues of all members of staff including non-Catholics can make a valuable and treasured contribution to the quality of the school's life and ethos.

Education is for the sake of human flourishing and therefore our approach to education will, of necessity, depend on our understanding of that what this involves. Human flourishing is the aim of human life and consists in the shared enjoyment of emotional, cultural, intellectual and spiritual life and, in particular, the sustaining of true friendships. However, from the Christian perspective such flourishing is possible only because of Christ through whom we find friendship with God and the promise of eternal life. From a Christian perspective it is therefore inadequate to limit our view of the human person, and thus of education, to what can be known by reason and experience. There is much more to be said about human life that can only be said in the light of faith, for only in the mystery of Jesus Christ is the mystery of the human person fully revealed. Human persons are in fact destined for something higher and greater than can be known in this life: a supreme Common Good, which is nothing less than a share in the very life of God. The remainder of this book will seek to explore this Christian revelation of the human person and draw out its implications for Catholic education.

Human flourishing is the aim of human life and consists in the shared enjoyment of emotional, cultural, intellectual and spiritual life and, in particular, the sustaining of true friendships.

2. Christian Education,
What difference does Jesus make?

4. Who is Jesus?

Some pointers for making use of this chapter

This chapter includes material that may be useful for non-Christians who may have a false or even a caricatured idea of what it means for God to speak to people (or indeed a caricatured view of religion in general). It may also help Catholics and non-Catholic Christians understand the Catholic approach to the interpretation of the Scriptures. These materials would be useful in the context of catechesis for staff where this exists, or perhaps for INSET. The last section on spirituality could readily be used for 6th form assemblies, meditations and catechetics. The definitions in this chapter could also be used for group discussions, which could lead to Q&A sessions. The whistle-stop tour of the Scriptures could act as a refresher or a useful mental map for teachers (especially where their subject may allude to the Bible without having the opportunity to explore it directly – as with allusions to Scriptural themes in literature or to disputes about the Bible in history).

Curriculum Links

OCR

OCR Unit G571: AS Philosophy of Religion (God as Creator)

OCR Unit G573: AS Jewish Scriptures (overview)

OCR Unit G574: AS New Testament (overview)

OCR Unit G575: AS Developments in Christian Theology (Foundations of theology, Person of Christ)

OCR Unit G581: A2 Philosophy of Religion (Experience and Revelation)

OCR Unit G584: A2 New Testament (overview)

AQA

AQA RS AS Unit F Old Testament (RSS06)

AQA RS AS Unit G New Testament (RSS07)

AQA RS AS Unit K World Religions 2: Christianity (Christian Scriptures)

AQA RS A2 Unit 3 Studies in Religion (RST3D, RST3E, RST3F)

AQA RS A2 Unit 4 Religion and Human Experience (RST4B, RST4C)

AQA RS A2 Unit 3E New Testament (RST3E)

Edexcel

Unit 1 Area D: Christianity

Unit 1 Area I: New Testament

Unit 2 Area E: The Study of the Old Testament/Jewish Bible

Unit 2 Area F: The Study of the New Testament

Unit 2 Area G: The Study of Christianity and the Christian Church (Christian Belief and Practice)

Unit 3 Area I: New Testament (Christology)

Unit 4 Question 9: New Testament (The Person of Christ, teachings)

Has God spoken?

There is a world which is an ordered whole, a cosmos not a chaos, with a common origin and common laws and processes. On our planet (and perhaps on others) this world has given rise to life, and on our planet (and perhaps on others) among the rich diversity of life there has appeared a form that is reflective and questioning, and thus in human beings (and perhaps in other ways) the universe has become aware of itself. Many philosophers in different ages have seen in the existence of the world, and in its order, and in the vitality of life, and in the light of reason, evidence of an ultimate source of all being, all order, all life, and all understanding. This they have called the One, the Supreme Being, the Creator, or more simply, God.

Many philosophers in different ages have seen in the existence of the world, and in its order, and in the vitality of life, and in the light of reason, evidence of an ultimate source of all being, all order, all life, and all understanding.

Yet even if some exceptional minds can come to know of God in this way, and can do so without error and without projecting their own limited understanding onto God, this kind of theoretical knowledge is only of limited use. For it is not enough to know that there is a God 'out there somewhere' and that there is meaning to the world somehow. Our needs are more immediate than that. We need to know how to live and we need help to live and we need hope in the face of loss and the difficulties of life. Human persons need something more than 'the God of the philosophers'. What we need is a revelation from God.

Revelation is the knowledge that creatures can have of God based on a word that God has spoken to them. It is the claim of Judaism, inherited by Christianity and by other religious traditions that are spiritual heirs of Judaism, that God, the Creator, has provided for this human need by speaking in history. The idea of God 'speaking' is, of course, a metaphor. The Creator of all things is not an animal with a mouth or vocal cords. To say that God has spoken is to say that certain events or actions or thoughts

Revelation is the knowledge that creatures can have of God based on a word that God has spoken to them.

or words in the life of rational creatures distinctively reveal to them the will or mind of the Creator. All of history and everything that happens is sustained by the Creator, but there are some particular moments that reveal the Divine meaning of things and that answer the creature's need for Divine guidance. This is what we mean by saying that God has spoken.

How could anyone have confidence that God was speaking to him or her? And even if someone did believe that he or she had a message from God, how could others believe it? Part of the answer to these questions is that, as well as giving the messenger the gift and the responsibility of having a message to deliver, God gives others the gift of believing the message. God is at work both in the one speaking with authority and in the one listening with faith. This gift (or 'theological virtue') of faith will be explored in the next chapter. Another part of the answer is that revelation is never given only to an individual. In the Jewish and Christian understanding it is not only that individuals are strengthened and inspired by God to speak 'the word of God'. More fundamentally, God shapes a people and a history, a community and a tradition, so that any new word from God is not entirely new. It also makes sense in relation to what has gone before. This is not to say that the community is always correct and the awkward individual always misguided. Frequently the prophets have been awkward individuals who have shamed the community that would not heed their words. However, their words have typically reminded the community of what it ought to have known: moral or religious truths that were present in the shared tradition but that had become neglected or distorted.

Truthful words have the ability to inspire in a variety of ways and this is all the more so of words that are written under the inspiration of God.

The idea of a revelation from God does not require a sacred text. Actions can speak louder than words, and words themselves can be spoken and believed and passed on without being written down. Nevertheless, what people treasure they want to protect and pass on. Hence the word of God spoken through events and through words has come to be written in sacred texts. This pattern is common in many religions making claim to divine revelation, not only Judaism and Christianity. Once the word is written then it becomes subject to different interpretations, by official and unofficial interpreters, and may be used in new ways by a new generation. Truthful words have the ability to inspire in a variety of ways and this is all the more so of words that are written under the inspiration of God.

Section 2

To understand the Scriptures it is necessary to understand what kind of writings they are, what the human author meant to say, and what God was and is saying through these words.

A Christian education will be based on the belief not only that there is a God but that God has acted in history by choosing and forming the people of Israel, and giving to them a revelation, a word from God. This word of God is present in those sacred books of the Jewish people which Christians call the Old Testament. From a Christian perspective, the Old Testament is only fully understood in relation to the person of Jesus made known in the writings of the New Testament, and these are only fully understood in and by the Church, in the context of the Christian Tradition. However, by the same token, the teaching of the Church is to be understood in relation to the person of Jesus, and Jesus is to be understood as the fulfilment of the promises of the Old Testament. Jesus was born a Jew, a

> The word 'Christ' is the Greek equivalent of the Hebrew word 'Messiah' meaning 'the anointed one' and refers to the promised Saviour who would be King of the Jews and heir to the throne of David.

direct descent of King David, and all his disciples were Jewish. This is not to deny that God may have spoken to other peoples and at other times in many ways, but the Christian faith is based on the belief that God has spoken definitively in Jesus, the Saviour promised to the Jews. This is evident even in the word 'Christianity'. The word 'Christ' is the Greek equivalent of the Hebrew word 'Messiah' meaning 'the anointed one' and refers to the promised Saviour who would be King of the Jews and heir to the throne of David. Hence, Christian education should include at least some knowledge of the books of the Old Testament.

Theology: Interpreting the Scriptures

To understand the Scriptures it is necessary to understand what kind of writings they are, what the human author meant to say, and what God was and is saying through these words. The Scriptures are not intended as a guide to natural science and in these things they speak according to the customs of their time and place. They teach us not how the heavens go, but how to go to heaven: what is the meaning and destiny of human life. If we expect the Scriptures always to be polite and pious then we will be surprised. In addition to laws, and prayers and sensible advice the Scriptures include jealousy and violence, anguish and despair, erotic poetry and raw expressions of human grief. These are Divinely-inspired words but spoken to and for human beings, so they do not hide the realities of human life. This is one reason that it is important to become familiar with the Scriptures directly. The more one is familiar with the breadth of the Scriptures, the more passages will speak to the particular situation in which we find ourselves. They will often challenge our preconceptions. It is also important to remember that, as the Scriptures themselves say, 'no prophecy of Scripture is a matter of one's own interpretation' (2 Peter 1:20) but all interpretation must be measured against the understanding of the Church.

A whistle-stop tour through the Scriptures

What follows is a whistle-stop tour through the 46 Jewish books that are recognised by the Catholic Church as the Old Testament, from Genesis to Malachi.

The Bible begins with a kind of prehistory of the world. The first 11 chapters of the book of Genesis reveal some fundamental features of human beings and the relation of the world to God. They are not just concerned with one particular people and its history but with all people, with humanity as such. These chapters speak in a poetic way about creation, about sin, about the origin of culture and about the relationship between human beings and the natural world. They also form the preamble to the story of one particular people.

These stories, told in the book of Genesis, root the identity of the people with a call from God.

The beginning of the story of the Jewish people, and so of Christianity (and also of Islam), is the calling of Abram. He was a man from Ur of the Chaldees (in what we now call Iraq) who heard God calling him to leave his home and go to a new land. God gave him a new name, Abraham, and told him that even though he was an old man he would be the father of a great nation and that his wife, Sarah, would bear a son. This happened as it was promised and Abraham was granted a son, Isaac, who himself had two sons, Jacob and Esau. Jacob was renamed Israel and had twelve sons who were the origin of the twelve tribes of Israel. This cycle of stories of Abraham, Isaac and Jacob comprise the oldest element of the tradition of the Jewish people. The word 'Jewish' refers to the tribe of Judah who was one of the twelve sons of Jacob. These stories, told in the book of Genesis, root the identity of the people with a call from God.

Jacob struggling with an Angel

A recurring theme through this long history is the faithfulness of God who fulfils his promises and the waywardness of human beings, including that of David and his descendants.

The next four books of the Bible (Exodus, Leviticus, Numbers, and Deuteronomy) tell the story of the liberation of the people from Egypt and their return to the Promised Land. The people had settled in Egypt and originally they were made to feel welcome there, but later there arose a Pharaoh 'who knew not Joseph' (Exodus 1:8) and who treated the people with the suspicion with which immigrants are often treated, and they were forced to become slaves. The book of Exodus tells how God chose Moses as his servant, and how God saved the people, led them out of Egypt and gave them a law based on Ten Commandments. The Commandments were written on two stone tablets and kept in a box called the Ark of the Covenant. The next three books, Leviticus, Numbers and Deuteronomy, expand or repeat parts of this story and set out many specific laws and rituals. The first five books of the Bible together make a unified whole which Christians call the Pentateuch and Jews call the Torah (which means, 'the Law'). Modern scholars have seen many sources, layers and acts of editing and re-editing within these books but God, who is the Creator of all things, can speak through any number of human authors and editors. Jews and Christians take these books, in the form that we have them now, to be Divinely inspired. They are the foundation of the identity of the Jewish people and the most sacred writings of Judaism.

The next two books of the Bible tell the story of the re-conquest of the land (Joshua) and the time when Israel was a loose confederation of tribes before they were united under a single king (Judges.) These books are the background to the story of David, who became king of Judah, and of all the tribes of Israel. David also captured Jerusalem, made it his capital and brought the Ark of the Covenant there (1 and 2 Samuel.) The books of 1 and 2 Kings tell the subsequent history of the kings of Judah and of Israel, from David's son Solomon (who built a Temple to house the Ark) to the last king Jehoiachin, who died in exile in Babylon. The story is then retold in 1 and 2 Chronicles. (This pattern of retelling the same story to bring out the meaning is a common feature of the Scriptures.) The Book of Kings ends with Jerusalem captured, the Temple destroyed and the king in exile. This seemed to be the end of the people, but sixty years or so later the people were allowed to return to Jerusalem and rebuild the Temple (Ezra, Nehemiah.) A recurring theme through this long history is the faithfulness of God who fulfils his promises and the waywardness of human beings, including that of David and his descendants.

The history of the people is continued in 1 and 2 Maccabees, the last two history books in the Bible which tell of events just over a century before Christ. They tell of the attempt of a Greek ruler, Antiochus Epiphanes, to impose Greek customs on the Jewish people, and of the successful rebellion led by Judas Maccabeus, which restored the freedom of Jews to follow the Torah in their own land. The first two books of Maccabees are included in Catholic Bibles but were not accepted as Scripture within later Judaism and are often included in Protestant Bibles only in an appendix called the Apocrypha. Among these ten historical books are four books relating stories of individuals, Ruth, Tobit (in Catholic Bibles), Esther, and Judith (in Catholic Bibles) within this history.

The book of Job is unique in that it does not tell the story of an ancestor or a descendent of Abraham but of an Edomite, from the land of Uz. Job is a righteous

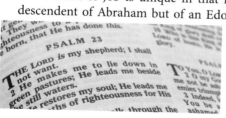

man who loses his wealth, his children and finally his health, and who is tempted to curse God, but does not do so. The book is an extended reflection on the problem of suffering.

After Job comes the Book of Psalms. These are 150 songs of prayer and worship, some dating as early as the time of David, some almost certainly used in the Temple, and used continually in Jewish and Christian prayers up to the present day. They express a range of emotions from celebration to sorrow, from hope to despair. Perhaps the most famous Psalm is a prayer for God's protection in the face of death, 'The Lord is my shepherd, I will not want…' (Psalm 23).

While King David was known as a singer of psalms, King Solomon was known for his wisdom (though with some ambivalence, for this wisdom came with a certain worldliness shown in his wealth and his many foreign wives) and there are five Biblical books which are known as Wisdom writings: Proverbs, Ecclesiastes, the Song of Songs (a song celebrating the erotic love of a man and a woman, which has been understood as expressing the love between the Lord and his people, between Christ and the Church, or between God and the soul), the book of Wisdom (only in Catholic Bibles) and Eccesiasticus, also called the book of Sirach (only in Catholic Bibles).

The remaining books of the Old Testament are by and/or about prophets. The prophets were messengers and each gave words of encouragement, warning, or condemnation for the people. Each had a particular character and spoke to the people of his time, but these prophecies are recorded because they were given also for the sake of later generations, including our own. A common theme in the prophets is the need for the people to repent of corrupt practices (and especially seeking after other gods and the oppression of the poor), and to return to the life-giving Torah. There are four 'major' prophets: Isaiah, Jeremiah (together with Lamentations and, in Catholic Bibles, Baruch), Ezekiel and Daniel (the book of Daniel has two extra chapters in Catholic Bibles). Finally there are twelve short books of 'minor' prophets: Hosea, Joel, Amos, Obadiah, Jonah, Micah, Nahum, Habakkuk, Zephaniah, Haggai, Zechariah, and Malachi. As well as calling the people to repent and turn to the Lord, the prophets also announced the promises of God including the promise of a saviour, the Messiah who would be a new king in the line of David, and the promise of a new age in which God's Spirit and God's presence would dwell with his people. These promises were fulfilled in the life, death, and resurrection of Jesus, though often in unexpected and paradoxical ways.

The Books of the Old Testament
Catholics accept as Holy Scripture the 46 books of the people of Israel, the Old Testament:

The Pentateuch: Genesis, Exodus, Leviticus, Numbers, Deuteronomy

The historical books: Joshua, Judges, Ruth, 1 Samuel, 2 Samuel, 1 Kings, 2 Kings, 1 Chronicles, 2 Chronicles, Ezra, Nehemiah, Tobit, Judith, Esther, 1 Maccabees, 2 Maccabees

The wisdom books: Job, Psalms, Proverbs, Ecclesiastes, Song of Solomon, Wisdom, Sirach

The prophetic books: Isaiah, Jeremiah, Lamentations, Baruch, Ezekiel, Daniel, Hosea, Joel, Amos, Obadiah, Jonah, Micah, Nahum, Habakkuk, Zephaniah, Haggai, Zechariah, Malachi

Seven of these books (Tobit, Judith, Wisdom, Sirach, Baruch, and 1 and 2 Maccabees) and parts of two others (Esther and Daniel) are not accepted as Scripture by modern Jews and are not found in Protestant Bibles, though they are sometimes included in an appendix called the '**apocrypha**'. The Catholic term for these books is '**deuterocanonical**'. They were written only a short time before Christ and seemed to some to be too recent to be sacred. However, these books were accepted by many of the Jews of Jesus' own day, especially those who became the first generation of Christians. This list of 46 books was the Old Testament known to Augustine and it is this list which was accepted as authoritative by the Council of Trent (1545-1563).

Section 2

The Word made flesh

In addition to the books of the Old Testament, Christians have their own Scriptures, the New Testament comprising four accounts of the life, death, and resurrection of Jesus (the Gospels according to Matthew, Mark, Luke and John). Also an account of the early Church (the Acts of the Apostles), 21 letters by Paul and other apostolic writers, and the Book of Revelation, which includes a vision of the end of the world.

The Books of the New Testament

There are 27 books in the New Testament.

The Gospels: Matthew, Mark, Luke, John

The Acts of the Apostles

The letters: Romans, 1 Corinthians, 2 Corinthians, Galatians, Ephesians, Philippians, Colossians, 1 Thessalonians, 2 Thessalonians, 1 Timothy, 2 Timothy, Titus, Philemon, Hebrews, James, 1 Peter, 2 Peter, 1 John, 2 John, 3 John, Jude

The Book of Revelation

Because Christians also have sacred books, it might be imagined that these books are for Christians what the Torah is for Jews, the basis of revelation, the place where the word of God is most fully revealed. However, to think this would be to make a mistake. While both the Old Testament and the New Testament are held sacred by Christians as containing the word of God, for the Christian faith, the Word of God is most fully revealed not in any book but in a human being, Jesus Christ. Jesus the living person was and is the Word of God: the words of the New Testament are the word of God in a secondary sense. As it says in the letter to the Hebrews, 'In many and various ways God spoke of old to our fathers by the prophets but in these last days he has spoken to us by a Son' (Hebrew 1:1-2), or in that memorable phrase from the Gospel according to John, 'the Word became flesh and dwelt among us' (John 1:14).

Jesus was born in Bethlehem, a village quite close to Jerusalem, and was brought up in the village of Nazareth, in the northern region of Galilee. The Gospels according to Matthew and Luke tell us that Jesus had a miraculous birth, being born of a virgin, Mary; nevertheless, his early life was hidden from the public. Jesus began his public ministry in a remarkable way, by seeking out John the Baptist and asking to be baptised. John the Baptist was a prophetic preacher, very like some of the Old Testament prophets, who challenged people to turn away from their sinful ways and show their repentance

Section 2

by being immersed in the River Jordan. John recognised that Jesus was a holy man and did not understand why he wanted to be baptised. Much later, people would realise it was because Jesus would die in order to take away the sins of the world, but at the time, like many things that Jesus did, it was not understood.

After he had been baptised Jesus called followers to him and named twelve disciples who would be his Apostles, the first of whom, Simon, he renamed Cephas (in Greek, Peter) which means 'rock'. As the people of Israel were formed from twelve sons of Jacob so the twelve Apostles would be the beginning of a new community. Jesus preached to people, often in parables that forced them to reflect on what he was saying. He also healed sick people and set free people who were afflicted with demons. He attracted controversy for healing people on the Sabbath, which is a day of rest, and for preaching against the hypocrisy of the religious leaders. He also scandalised people by mixing with notorious sinners and was accused of blasphemy when he told people that their sins were forgiven. If a sin is an offence against God, then only God can forgive sins.

Eventually through the betrayal of one of his own disciples and with the connivance of the Jewish religious leaders, Jesus was handed over to the Roman colonial authorities. He was tortured and executed for sedition, on the grounds that he claimed to be a king. Most of his disciples fled, apart from his mother, some of his female followers, and a disciple whom the Gospel according to John calls 'the beloved disciple' (John 20:2). The crucifixion was the most desolate moment for his followers and seemed to be the end of all hope, just as centuries before the destruction of the Temple and the death of the king in exile had seemed to be the end of the Jewish nation.

Christians recognised Jesus as the saviour not just of Israel, but of the whole world: not just a new David or a new Moses but a new Adam, a new beginning for humanity.

These events, at least in outline, are not disputed by historians. It is not disputed that Jesus was known as a miracle worker and as a controversial preacher who antagonised the religious authorities. It is not disputed that he was executed under the orders of the Roman Prefect, Pontius Pilate, or that he was crucified and buried. What happened next is at the core of Christian faith. Some of those who had witnessed the death of Jesus went three days later to complete the burial customs, but found that the body was not there. While they were unsure of what to make of this, Jesus himself appeared to them in a way that was both physical and not like an ordinary body. There were many resurrection appearances, only a few of which are described in the Gospels. Having been scattered and afraid, the community gathered together again and experienced a transforming power, the presence of the Spirit of God, as promised by the prophets. Having been a movement confined to Jews living in Galilee and Judea, the Christian Church spread through the known world, attracting first Jews and then increasingly gentiles or non-Jews, again in fulfilment of prophecies in the Old Testament. Christians recognised Jesus as the saviour not just of Israel, but of the whole world: not just a new David or a new Moses but a new Adam, a new beginning for humanity.

Truly God & truly human

Christianity, like Judaism, is based on the belief that God has provided for human beings a way to discover the meaning of human life and indeed of the existence of everything, and has provided the help we need to live life as we should. This God did first by forming a particular people to whom he spoke repeatedly in history and by the prophets. Christians believe that this revelation to the Jews was fulfilled by the sending of Jesus who, although he was a Jew, and ministered primarily to Jews, gave his life to reconcile the whole world to God, Jews and gentiles, and to found a community that would include people of every nation. The Divine revelation which was particular, and had to be particular if it was to create a community and a tradition, was always destined to be universal and it became universal though the person of Jesus. In Jesus the revelation of God, that is, the Word, was spoken in a way that was not just for one person or one people but was for all humanity. Jesus is the Word made flesh – he was not only one who spoke the word but he was and is the Word: from the first his whole identity, his life and character and actions and suffering, expressed in a human way the life of God.

In Jesus the revelation of God, that is, the Word, was spoken in a way that was not just for one person or one people but was for all humanity.

From the earliest times, as witnessed in the writings of the New Testament, Christians have struggled to grasp fully the identity of Jesus as the Word of God and beloved Son of God who is at the same time the promised 'son of man' and the new Adam. They have been insistent that Jesus was and is (now in a glorified way) a human being, born of a woman, sharing human nature, having the same flesh and blood, the same mental and emotional powers, the same physical needs, the same liability to

The 'Incarnation' is the word Christians use to reflect the mysterious truth that, in Jesus, God became human, without ceasing to be God and without overwhelming his humanity.

pain and suffering as other human beings. Jesus was like us in all things but sin (which is not an authentic feature of our humanity but is precisely our failure to be fully human). At the same time Christians have insisted that Jesus is really God among us: not simply a friend of God or a spokesman for God but truly God and truly human, God living a human life. Christians therefore came to see the relationship between Father and Son as something eternal, an eternal love of parent and child within God, and this eternal love becomes visible when the child, the eternal beloved Son, takes on a human nature and becomes human. The 'Incarnation' is the word Christians use to reflect the mysterious truth that, in Jesus, God became human, without ceasing to be God and without overwhelming his humanity.

Theology: Who is Jesus?

Over the centuries Christians have fought sometimes bitter battles among themselves against those who denied that Jesus was truly human (Docestists and Gnostics), or against those who denied he was truly God (Ebionites and Arians) or those who confused the human and Divine natures (Monophysites) or those who separated Jesus into two distinct persons (Nestorians). It is easy to think that that these people were arguing about words and forgetting the message of Christianity. However, the words mattered to people because it matters who Jesus is and what he has done. It is because Jesus is at once Divine and human that *he was able to save us by becoming one of us*. Christians have sometimes been lacking in charity in the way they have guarded and explored this mysterious truth, and have sometimes mistreated those who disagreed. Nevertheless, they have been right to see the importance of this staggering revelation, that God has become one of us. God has shared our joys and suffering, and known them not only as God but also as we do: he has given us hope in a human way through becoming human.

The incarnation also reinforces the Jewish view that human beings are bodily beings. Human beings are at once spiritual and bodily and even the hope of life after death is a hope for some radical transformation of the body, a new body, as Jesus possessed after his resurrection. Hope is not hope for an escape from the body as the philosopher Plato thought, as though we were really souls trapped in bodies longing for the end of our prison term.

The body is not a prison outside of us; it is us. This is why the Catholic religion involves not just words but physical signs, symbols and rituals, touch and taste, water and oil, bread and wine. The faith is tied to, and in the world: it is not just about ideas. The central prayer of the Church is the Celebration of Mass, the Eucharist or last supper which Jesus instituted the night before he died, and in which the bread and wine, while retaining the appearances of bread and wine, become his body and blood. The resurrection of Jesus *is* the resurrection of a body and the presence of Jesus in the Mass is the presence of that body. Christianity has much to say about the human spirit, and the next section will explore the Christian understanding of 'spirituality' (which concerns the presence of God's Spirit within us) but the Christian faith does not separate the spiritual life (in either sense) from the life of the body. The Word was made flesh.

The unity of the human person as body and soul is hugely important in thinking about ethics.

The unity of the human person as body and soul is hugely important in thinking about ethics. For example, it is a mistake to think of the body as something outside us and therefore as property which is can be used in any way we choose. What happens to the body happens to us. There is a language of the body which already has meaning and cannot be used to say anything we want. There are different cultures that are more or less emotionally expressive, but sexual intimacy necessarily implies a rich human meaning. If this intimacy is sought without a context of love, then it is a kind of lie. 'A context of love' here implies both commitment to and responsibility for one another,

Section 2

and responsibility for the consequences of our actions. This is but one example of many ways in which we care for each other or fail to care for each other by how we treat our bodies and the bodies of others.

The Spiritual life

Jesus is the beloved Son of his heavenly Father, and the New Testament describes him both as son of man and as Son of God. However, the word used most often to describe Jesus, so much so that it almost begins to seem like a name rather than a title, is Christ. The word Christ means 'anointed one'. The Christ was the one anointed by God with power to be king and saviour of the people. A king is anointed with oil but this symbolises the more important anointing which is the power of the Holy Spirit. The promised Messiah is also the one who will bring a new age in which the Holy Spirit will be given to everyone.

The Christ is the Spirit-bearer who both acts with the power of the Holy Spirit and promises that he will send the Holy Spirit to give new life to the community of believers. The way Jesus describes the Holy Spirit makes it clear that the Spirit is a distinct person, not just a way to speak of the presence of God. For this reason Christians describe God as a Trinity of Father, Son and Holy Spirit: the Father begetting the Son, and the Father and Son breathing forth the Spirit, through all eternity. The Holy Spirit is God.

The event most associated with the coming of the Holy Spirit is Pentecost, after the resurrection and the ascension of Jesus into heaven, when the disciples were suddenly filled with joy and began to praise God in many different languages. This event shows how the Spirit is associated with gifts (especially the gifts of speech and understanding), with confidence, and with joy and vitality. Most of all the Spirit is associated with life, because of the association of breath with life. Hence the Nicene Creed calls the Holy Spirit, 'the Lord, the Giver of life'. The Gospel is the 'good news' that, through the death and resurrection of Christ, God has reconciled the world to himself, has overcome sin and death, and has sent the Holy Spirit among us to bring us eternal life.

Baptism of Christ

In the New Testament the word 'spirit' is used in different ways. It is sometimes used to mean a part of a human being, a person's spiritual soul, and sometimes to mean the Holy Spirit, God who dwells in the heart of the believer. Occasionally both senses occur in the same sentence, as when Paul says 'When we cry, "Abba! Father!" it is the Spirit himself bearing witness with our spirit that we are children of God' (Romans 8:15-16). This difference reminds us that the presence of the Holy Spirit is an extra gift given to us: something more than our natural human powers, more even than the powers of the mind. In this context, sometimes Christians speak of 'the grace of God'. The word 'grace' means 'free gift' and refers to the help we receive freely from God.

Section 2

It refers especially to the gift by which we live well and by which we become friends of God. It is important to recognise that this 'grace' is not a *thing* but the presence of a person, the Holy Spirit dwelling within us. It is a personal presence with us and in us that inspires us to do and be more and, in particular, that inspires us to love God. We are often less aware of the Spirit as a distinct person because the Holy Spirit is always with us and in us, encouraging us to look outward, to others, or to Jesus and the Father.

> The Gospel is the 'good news' that, through the death and resurrection of Christ, God has reconciled the world to himself, has overcome sin and death, and has sent the Holy Spirit among us to bring us eternal life.

These characteristics of the Spirit explain both the meaning and the attraction of the term 'spirituality'. The word 'spirituality', in a Christian sense, is the transforming effect of the Holy Spirit upon the person as the person makes his or her way to God by the way that is Christ. There are many and diverse patterns and exemplars of Christian spirituality, some more austere, some more imaginative, some more stable, some more informal, but all will include these fundamental elements: the Holy Spirit, the person of Christ, transformation, the spiritual way, that is, the journey or 'pilgrimage' to God. Whereas religion is a visible set of practices and traditions and a community of belief, to speak of spirituality is to focus on its effect in the heart of the individual. From a Christian perspective it is very important to assert that the Spirit is active outside as well as inside, in the visible and in the communal, not only in the private and the solitary. As G.K Chesterton remarked with characteristic passion, 'That Jones shall worship the god within him turns out ultimately to mean that Jones shall worship Jones... Christianity came into the world firstly in order to assert with violence that a man had not only to look inwards, but to look outwards, to behold with astonishment and enthusiasm a divine company and a divine captain' (*Orthodoxy* ch. V.)

> The word 'grace' means 'free gift' and refers to the help we receive freely from God. It refers especially to the gift by which we live well and by which we become friends of God.

Nevertheless, there is also a place for the solitary, and for being attentive to the Holy Spirit active within the human heart. It may indeed be the case that someone practises outwardly but is not allowing the Spirit to work within his or her life. On the other hand, it may be that the Spirit is active in the inner life of someone who does not belong to a believing community and who may even be alienated from the external forms of religion. Jesus said of the Holy Spirit, 'the wind blows where it chooses' (John 3:8), and so God is not restricted by the limits of visible religious practice. Christians should therefore be respectful and supportive of those who are searching honestly for a spiritual way to live, but equally should be ready to respond positively and without embarrassment when someone is aware of a call to 'take it further' and seek instruction in the Catholic faith.

> The word 'spirituality', in a Christian sense, is the transforming effect of the Holy Spirit upon the person as the person makes his or her way to God by the way that is Christ.

Section 2

The word spirituality recognises the personal, inner, and existential aspect of religion: the aspect that is both more immediate and freer. It is interesting that even the Department for Education recognises that 'every state-funded school must offer a curriculum which is balanced and broadly based and which promotes the *spiritual*, moral, cultural, mental and physical development of pupils' (*National Curriculum in England* 2.1). On the other hand this very use by a government source may seem to confirm the impression that the word 'spiritual' is undefined and unchallenging, or at worst represents a kind of thin substitute for religion or even a form of syncretism (an ad hoc combination of different elements drawn from different religions and philosophies), ignoring not only the communal and the traditional but also the bodily aspects of human life. However, Christian teachers should not be afraid to use the terms 'spiritual' and 'spirituality' if at the same time they provide their own distinctive account of spirituality and of the different Christian approaches to spirituality. It is necessary to use the plural (approaches to spirituality) because through the centuries, different saints and schools have developed a variety of approaches to spirituality, from the regular and communal (like that of Saint Benedict), to the starkly minimal (like that of Saint John of the Cross), to the richly imaginative (like that of Saint Teresa of Avila) and different people at different times may find one or another of these approaches helpful. While some Christians are happy to speak of spirituality some prefer to speak of holiness. Holiness is the effect of the Holy Spirit in a human person to make someone 'holy', which means, 'set apart' for the service of God.

> Holiness is the effect of the Holy Spirit in a human person to make someone 'holy', which means, 'set apart' for the service of God.

From a Christian perspective it is very important to assert that the Spirit is active outside as well as inside, in the visible and in the communal, not only in the private and the solitary.

The diversity of approaches to spirituality, and indeed the diversity in the personalities of the saints, shows that holiness can be expressed in different ways. Every Christian is called to become holy in his or her own way. Being holy implies being perfect in the sense of dedicated *wholly* to God. If the Holy Spirit unites us to God it must be the whole of us that is united to God. There is no part of us that is untouched by grace.

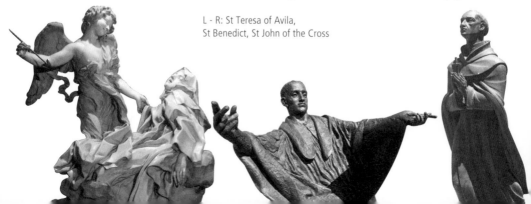

L - R: St Teresa of Avila,
St Benedict, St John of the Cross

5. The Virtues Transformed

Some pointers for making use of this chapter

This chapter develops discussion of the virtues (already explored in chapter 2) in an explicitly Christian context. It therefore fits with activities aimed at catechetical teaching. This material could inform assemblies but might be embedded further if used for activities in tutor groups and chaplaincy-led activities. Such a context would allow time for group discussion, focused prayer and meditation on this particular theme. It naturally fits as the complement to general discussion of the virtues building on the introduction to virtue thinking. Hence it may be more appropriate to introduce the material here later in the school. From the perspective of the curriculum this approach presents a richer and more subtle account of religious ethics, developing a particular 'secular' approach (virtue ethics as understood in conjunction with the complementary themes of natural law, human rights, and moral duties) rather than presenting 'religious ethics' as a disconnected alternative system of ethics.

Curriculum links

OCR

OCR Unit G571: AS Philosophy of Religion

OCR Unit G572: AS Religious Ethics

OCR Unit G582: A2 Religious Ethics

AQA

AQA A2 Unit 3A Religion and Ethics (RST3A) (Virtues, Religious Views)AQA Philosophy Unit 1 PHIL1 An Introduction to Philosophy 1 (Nietzsche)

AQA Philosophy Unit 3 PHIL3 Key Themes in Philosophy (Moral philosophy, Virtues, Philosophy of Religion)

AQA Philosophy Unit 4 PHIL4 Philosophical Problems (Nietzsche)

Edexcel

Unit 2 Area F: The Study of the New Testament (New Testament morality)

Unit 2 Area G: The Study of Christianity and the Christian Church (Christian Belief and Practice)

Unit 3 Area B: Ethics (Virtue ethics)

Unit 4 Question 2: Ethics (Moral theory, virtues)

Unit 4 Question 4: Christianity (Ethics and religions)

Strength in weakness

The coming of Christ has profound implications for the understanding of education and has shaped the practice of education throughout Christian history. Subsequent chapters will explore these implications, especially but not only in relation to Catholic schools. The present chapter considers the impact of Christianity for the understanding and cultivation of the virtues. It is necessary to return to consideration of the virtues because they played such as significant role in the account of education developed in the first part of this book. That account emphasised the importance of cultivating the virtues for the *integral formation of the human person*, which, it was argued, is the aim of education broadly conceived. While school education may be more directly concerned with the liberation of the person through the development of the mind, this also requires intellectual virtues, and presupposes a community within which the moral virtues are practised and promoted. Furthermore, schools also have a role in assisting or supporting parents in the broader task of educating their children including in the development of moral character. It seems an adequate account of education must consider the virtues.

What light does Christ shed on the task of cultivating the virtues? It is noticeable that Jesus did not seek out people who were already well-practised in the virtues but sought out people who felt lost or helpless, who knew themselves to be sinners. So also, the hope and forgiveness that Jesus promised comes from outside, as a free gift. It is true that the encounter with Jesus and the gift of the Holy Spirit has a transforming effect on the character of the person and that this effect can be described in terms of Christian virtues. Nevertheless, it is noticeable that the *source* of these virtues is not (at least not primarily or in the first instance) human effort. They are effects of the grace of God.

In general, the story of the gospel is not a story of people slowly acquiring good habits by practice and education; it is a drama of human sin and Divine forgiveness, of falling and of being rescued, of the intervention of God through his Son and the power of the Holy Spirit. This not only changes how someone gets the virtues. It also has a subtle effect on *what the virtues are like* when they have been infused by grace.

While for Aristotle and other classical authors the archetype of courage was the soldier fighting bravely despite the risk to his life, for Christianity the archetype of courage is the martyr who endures suffering and death rather than betray the faith. The martyrs include not just physically strong men in the prime of life but those who may be weaker physically but who show courage in the face of suffering. Prominent among the martyrs are women and children, the very young and the very old. While the courage of a soldier is attributed to his spiritedness, strength of character, and training, the endurance of the martyrs is attributed to a power that comes from God. Indeed the very weakness of the martyrs, in human terms, bears witness to the power of God 'by which, in our weakness you perfect your power and on the feeble bestow strength to bear you witness' (Preface of martyrs).

The power of God by which, in our weakness you perfect your power and on the feeble bestow strength to bear you witness. Preface of martyrs

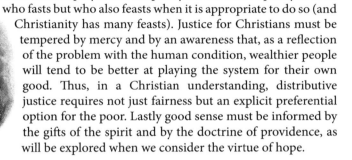

Similarly the image of temperateness for Christians is not the athlete who eats and exercises in the measure of the health and fitness of the body, but is the monk or nun who lives a life of prayer and simplicity for the sake of purity of soul, who fasts but who also feasts when it is appropriate to do so (and Christianity has many feasts). Justice for Christians must be tempered by mercy and by an awareness that, as a reflection of the problem with the human condition, wealthier people will tend to be better at playing the system for their own good. Thus, in a Christian understanding, distributive justice requires not just fairness but an explicit preferential option for the poor. Lastly good sense must be informed by the gifts of the spirit and by the doctrine of providence, as will be explored when we consider the virtue of hope.

Nietzsche

Myth: Christianity is a mean-spirited religion

The philosopher Friedrich Nietzsche (d. 1900) was right to see that the spirit of Christian virtue was very different from the ancient pagan virtues. However, he was wrong to see Christianity as an envious or mean-spirited religion. It is rather a generous-spirited religion because it does not measure achievement over and against others or see external success as necessary for self-worth. Self-worth is found in the first place through knowing that each person is created by God and possesses the image of God. This helps us recognise the dignity of the person in ourselves and in others, even when it is obscured by sin. More significant still, God has shown his love for each human being even to the extent of dying for our sake while we were sinners. Christians can take confidence from this, but it is a confidence that is based not on our own achievements but on the power of God. Similarly, the acceptance of God's grace inspires large-heartedness, but it is a form of greatness that expresses itself in a wish to serve others. This is what Jesus said: 'whoever would be great among you must be your servant' (Matthew 20:26).

Section 2

In addition to the transformation of the four cardinal virtues, theologians such as Augustine and Aquinas, drawing on the New Testament (1 Corinthians 13:13) identified three virtues that were distinctive to Christianity: faith, hope and love. These three 'theological virtues' will be discussed below, but before turning to distinctively Christian virtues it is reasonable to ask how the gospel affects our understanding of the vices.

Deadly sins

As the account we give of virtue is transformed by the coming of Christ, so also it is necessary to revisit the understanding of vice. Some elements of the classical account of the vices can still be maintained. It is true, and important, that vices characteristically represent extreme, partial, or one-sided dispositions toward the good and that virtue characteristically lies between opposite vices. Aristotle's insight that courage is a mean between cowardice and recklessness remains valid.

'For from within, out of the heart of man, come evil thoughts, fornication, theft, murder, adultery, coveting, wickedness, deceit, licentiousness, envy, slander, pride, foolishness. All these evil things come from within, and they defile a man' (Mark 7:21-23).

It is also true, and important, that vices like virtues are dispositions to action. They are not actions but they are shaped by our actions and they incline us to action. Whereas some accounts of morality are concerned only with actions (or only with rules about action), the concepts of virtue and vice trace actions back to their source in the dispositions of the human character. It is noticeable that Jesus, in his moral teaching, spoke not only about actions, and about which actions where permitted by the Law, but also spoke about the dispositions that gave rise to action. When asked to rebuke his disciples for eating without ritually washing their hands Jesus replied that what makes someone unclean comes from within, 'For from within, out of the heart of man, come evil thoughts, fornication, theft, murder, adultery, coveting, wickedness, deceit, licentiousness, envy, slander, pride, foolishness. All these evil things come from within, and they defile a man' (Mark 7:21-23). The idea that it is the dispositions of the human heart that give rise to good and evil deeds, and that to do well we need God to give us a change of heart, is one that is already found in the Old Testament. What Jesus adds to this, in his teaching and in his life, is that this change of heart is given through our faith in him.

There is a clear overlap between this Scriptural concept of the human heart and the classical account of virtues and vices. Where there is a difference is that, according to Aristotle, the virtues and vices are formed by repeated actions. The dispositions that are built up are stable and endure over time. In contrast, the Scriptures show the dispositions of the human heart as more changeable than this, more liable to temptation (and sin), more open to conversion (through grace).

'sin is crouching at the door; its desire is for you, but you must master it'
Genesis 4:7

The good news of the gospel is that Jesus is the Saviour of the world, of the whole human race, but this also implies the not-so-good news that the human race needs saving. Thus Christians and Jews speak not only of vice, and of offences against Sins are actions that are incompatible with the love of God and they are deadly (or 'mortal') inasmuch as they cut us off from the life that comes from God.

justice, but of sin which is an offence against God. Sins are actions that are incompatible with the love of God and they are deadly (or 'mortal') inasmuch as they cut us off from the life that comes from God. As well as mortal sins, which cut us off entirely from friendship with God, there are acts that fail to express love, but that only concern something trivial, or that are excusable, for example because we were honestly and reasonably unaware of the consequences of our actions. An act that fails to express love but that is trivial or excusable Catholics call a 'venial sin'. Such acts are not commendable but they do not cut us off from friendship with God. On the other hand, it is not only the personal mortal sins that we commit that can alienate us from God. From our origin the human race has been alienated and needed to be rescued, restored, forgiven, not due to what we had done individually, but due to a different kind of sin, a sin that we have inherited along with our human nature. There is something wrong at the root of the human condition, as it exists now, that affects every human being coming into the world and that alienates us from God and from one another. The one exception is Jesus Christ who, while fully human, is also God among us who came to save us from sin and death. Even Mary, the most perfect of the saints, needed to be rescued from this fallen condition, albeit in her case God accomplished this by sanctifying her in the very moment of her conception. This primeval alienation from God into which each of us is born is what Catholics call 'original sin'.

> An act that fails to express love but that is trivial or excusable Catholics call a 'venial sin'.

> This primeval alienation from God into which each of us is born is what Catholics call 'original sin'.

'like God, knowing good and evil' Genesis 3.5

The murder of Abel by his brother Cain.

As a Christian understanding of virtue will emphasise the need to rely on God's grace, so a Christian understanding of vice will recognise the weakness of the present human condition and the danger of falling into sin. In the book of Genesis, when God sees that Cain is angry, he warns him that 'sin is couching at the door; its desire is for you, but you must master it' (Genesis 4:7). Cain does not heed this warning but, in anger, kills his brother. This pattern of trial or temptation is a constant theme of the Scriptures, beginning with the story of Adam and Eve who were tempted by the promise that they would be 'like God, knowing good and evil' (Genesis 3:5). They fell and this was the beginning of a history in which God's chosen people repeatedly sin and turn away from the path to life.

A Christian account of vice will therefore include a greater sense of the universal need to guard against temptations, and indeed the need to pray not to be led into temptation. The Gospels describe how Jesus was tempted and was victorious and this teaches us that it is possible, by the grace of God, to overcome trials and temptations. Nevertheless, such a victory always relies on the grace of God and is not based on, or guaranteed by, previous good actions. The Christian attitude should therefore be, 'let anyone who thinks that he stands take heed lest he fall' (1 Corinthians 10:12).

'let anyone who thinks that he stands take heed lest he fall' 1 Corinthians 10:12

It follows from this that there are some vices that are particularly dangerous from a Christian perspective, because they prevent us from seeing the dangers of sin or from seeking the help we need from God. Among these the foremost is pride. There are various lists of sins or vices in the Scriptures and in the Christian Tradition. Perhaps the most well-known are the 'seven deadly sins' listed by Pope Gregory the Great: pride, avarice, envy, anger, lust, gluttony, and apathy. What is most noteworthy is that first place in this list, and in nearly all such lists, is given to the sin of pride.

the 'seven deadly sins' listed by Pope Gregory the Great: pride, avarice, envy, anger, lust, gluttony, and apathy.

Pride is based on a false idea that we can be independent of God and of others and that this is what we should want to be: a strong person of independent means who is not beholden to anyone. Pride contradicts the fundamental Jewish and Christian belief that the world and everything in it has been created by God, that our own existence is a gift and that all the good things in life are given to us by God. Pride is also a failure to acknowledge the doctrine of the fall, the realisation that human beings have rejected and neglected and destroyed these gifts, and that whenever we sin we play our own part in this great fall. Finally, and most significantly, pride is a failure to recognise the love by which Jesus offered his life so that human beings could be reconciled to God. This failure is the worst because it prevents us from accepting the forgiveness and help that would bring us life and happiness. It is like a drowning man who refuses to take the hand that is stretched out to save him: unless we accept that we are drowning, we cannot be saved.

Teaching the faith

Vices are perhaps easier to identify than virtues, but the aim of the moral life (and hence an aim of education) is not just avoiding vice but acquiring virtue. What, then, are the virtues of a Christian? In addition to the transformation of the four cardinal virtues, Christians have put forward three distinctively Christian virtues, known as the theological virtues: faith, hope and love (1 Corinthians 13:13) and to complement these, seven gifts of the Holy Spirit that are needed to guide and prompt the virtues.

Peter walks on water to Christ but doubts

Perhaps the most problematic of these three for a Catholic school in a modern context is the idea that faith is a virtue. A school which is based on the Christian faith should obviously teach and promote this virtue. But if faith is a gift, how can it be taught? And how is the teaching of faith to occur fairly and sensitively in a context where not all staff share this faith and not all pupils share this faith?

The theological virtue of Faith is the gift of God which enables us to place our trust in God and to believe what has been revealed as a word from God. An act of faith, in the Christian sense, will require or imply believing certain things - believing that God has spoken in history or that

> The theological virtue of Faith is the gift of God which enables us to place our trust in God and to believe what has been revealed as a word from God.

Jesus died to bring forgiveness to the world - but what makes faith a *virtue* is not the fact of having these beliefs but is the attitude by which the person comes to believe. Faith is a kind of trusting. It is placing trust in God and believing something because it is a word from God.

Peter coming to Christ as an image of faith

And in the fourth watch of the night he came to them, walking on the sea. But when the disciples saw him walking on the sea, they were terrified, saying, 'It is a ghost!' And they cried out for fear. But immediately he spoke to them, saying, 'Take heart, it is I; have no fear.' And Peter answered him, 'Lord, if it is you, bid me come to you on the water.' He said, 'Come.' So Peter got out of the boat and walked on the water and came to Jesus; but when he saw the wind, he was afraid, and beginning to sink he cried out, 'Lord, save me.' Jesus immediately reached out his hand and caught him, saying to him, 'O man of little faith, why did you doubt?' And when they got into the boat, the wind ceased. And those in the boat worshiped him, saying, 'Truly you are the Son of God.'

Section 2

It is possible to be mistaken about whether God has spoken or whether this or that word is really from God, and through history there have been many, and sometimes contradictory, claims that this or that message is from God. Nevertheless, once people with faith come to believe that a particular message is indeed from God, that it is God's word, they will trust God that it is true. They will believe this word because they trust in God.

According to the Christian gospel, faith is a gift - an effect of God within us. Thus if God speaks and someone believes the word, it is not only the speaking of the word that is an act of God (through a prophet or through a holy book or through the person of Jesus) but the believing is also an act of God. The Holy Spirit who dwells in the heart moves the believer to enable him or her to accept the word. It should also be noted that the Holy Spirit is present not only in believers as individuals but in the community, the Church, and this is an important way that people can test whether their belief is from God. Does it cohere with the way the community as a whole understands the Word? In particular, does our understanding cohere with the understanding of the bishops of the Church, who are in communion with each other and with the bishop of Rome, as this has been expressed through Christian history? Making a mistake about some matter of belief is not itself a failure of the virtue of faith - faith is not assessed by examination! Rather, faith is shown by the willingness to listen afresh to the Word and to be corrected by the community of faith. The object of the faith is credible and trustworthy precisely because it is not just a construct of my own mind or other human minds. The Word is believed by faith only if it is believed to be a word from outside, from God: a word given to supplement and sometimes to correct the achievements of the human mind.

Teaching can thus be an occasion for faith, but faith itself cannot be taught nor brought about by any inducement or technique. It is a gift of God. What can be learned and passed on is the Church's understanding of the Word of God. This knowledge is something that can be passed on even by those, or to those, who do not hold it as a matter of faith. However, the distinction between believing by faith and 'knowing about' creates a tension in particular in the teaching of Christian doctrine. It has already been noted that, in general, teachers may experience the problem of trying to 'serve two masters' in teaching to the assessment and teaching for the sake of knowledge and understanding. This is still more problematic with regard to Christian doctrine where what is aimed at is (or ought to be) not only knowledge or understanding but *an occasion for believing by faith.* Whereas modes of assessment may succeed or may fail in assessing important subjects of knowledge and understanding (hence being a possible source of tension for teachers) it is impossible even in principle for such modes to assess faith, nor should they seek to. What is required rather is an utterly different spirit by which children can be introduced to ideas not only as items for future assessment but as a message addressed to them in person. The challenge of a Catholic school may thus be not so much in teaching as in *not teaching* but rather creating space that is reflective, free, and open to grace.

Faith in the revelation of Christ also has implications for the understanding of the aim of education and how each subject fits into this overall aim. In subtle ways this should affect the teaching of all subjects: in the content of the curriculum (for many, though not all subjects), in the approach to teaching, and in the interrelation with other subjects. These themes will be explored in the last section of the book. At this point it is enough to note that the virtue of faith, where present, will transform not only religious education but education as such.

Hope & discernment

Between faith (which defines religion) and love (which is the heart of Christianity), hope is the least prominent of the three theological virtues and the least discussed, even by theologians. However, from the perspective of education it is arguably the most important of the virtues. Hope transforms the present by reference to the future. It gives sense and meaning to the present and inspires preparation and eagerness for that future. It provides education with its object - with the end towards which it strives. It might be objected that education is not only about a future good but is a good in the present. It is good to learn and to discover new things and to do so together with others, and the whole of life is or ought to be a process of learning. However, the same can be said of hope. As Augustine notes, hope not only looks to the future good but is a way of being happy now. The hopeful person has a direction and meaning in life in the present and can take pleasure from the present without fear while the person who despairs about the future finds it hard also to enjoy the present.

Augustine said 'You made us for yourself and our heart is restless until it rests in you' Confessions I.1

Hope is an emotion that is common to all people and even to other animals - the dog looks hopefully for his walk, the cat for her breakfast. What makes hope a distinctively Christian virtue is the object and basis of the hope. Of any hope one can always ask - what is it hope for? and what is it hope in? Christian hope is hope for God and hope in God. It is *hope for God* because God is our ultimate happiness, even if we do not always realise this. As Augustine said 'You made us for yourself and our heart is restless until it rests in you' (*Confessions* I.1). This happiness will include all we can be - our mind, our bodily life, our friendships - but ultimately it will be a return to our origin, our beginning and end. Furthermore, hope is *hope in God* because the basis of this hope is not our own abilities, or any human power, but is trust in the one who created us and who has a plan for our life. The theological virtue of hope enables us to face our own future and that of the whole world with the confidence that God has prepared a path for each of us through which we can come to happiness.

The theological virtue of hope enables us to face our own future and that of the whole world with the confidence that God has prepared a path for each of us through which we can come to happiness.

An effect of hope, in its Christian sense, is to provide an overall confidence that there is for each person a path in and through which he or she can find happiness (or we might say, can find himself or herself). It will be a task of education in its Christian sense to help people to discover the path to which God is calling them. Discernment is the process by which someone discovers the path to which he or she is being called by God. This process can sometimes be helped by a wise guide but it

Discernment is the process by which someone discovers the path to which he or she is being called by God.

would be a mistake to think that there is a mechanism or a technique for discovering or testing our vocation. The call of God is an act of God and comes as the Holy Spirit chooses, often surprising us. Sometimes it will become clear if we wait and listen for it, but sometimes God will interrupt our carefully laid plans and the path we thought was ours.

For this reason the virtue of hope (and the theological virtues in general) cannot be self-contained the way the cardinal virtues seem to be self-contained. The cardinal virtues are directed to a good that is seen and known. In contrast the theological virtues orient us to good that we do not see and to which we have access only though a personal relationship with God. Good sense is a virtue by which our reason guides us towards an end that we have in mind, but hope opens us up to an end which God has in mind for us. The theological virtues therefore need to be supplemented by further gifts of God that dispose us to be receptive to the promptings of God, so that we can discern what we should do in concrete situations, on the basis not of abstract principles or reasons, but of God's specific calling. The Catholic tradition lists seven such gifts: wisdom, understanding, counsel, fortitude, knowledge, piety, and fear of the Lord (based on Isaiah 11:2-3). Each in its own way is thought of as a way of being receptive to God in the present moment.

> The Catholic tradition lists seven such gifts: wisdom, understanding, counsel, fortitude, knowledge, piety, and fear of the Lord. Based on Isaiah 11:2-3

One of the most striking teachings of Jesus, and the most difficult to make sense of in relation to the cardinal virtues is the statement that we should take no thought for tomorrow, to what we will wear or what we should eat, but that, like the birds of the air and lilies of the field, we should rely on providence (Matthew 6:25-6:34). This seems to be unbelievably naïve and to stand in complete contradiction to sensible prudent planning for the future. Indeed it seems irresponsible. If young people were to follow this advice how quickly could they come to regret it? It should of course be noted that Jesus does not forbid people to make plans and prepare for the future. The teaching is directed against people being anxious about the future. 'Do not be anxious' (Matthew 6:25). Anxiety will not help one way or the other. Nevertheless, Jesus seems to give priority to trust in providence over planning for the future.

> 'Do not be anxious' Matthew (based on Isaiah 11:2-3)

Providence is the care and foresight by which God provides for the world and humanity so that things are able to achieve their end. The providence of God extends not only to species and to general laws but to each and every individual. Belief in providence does not negate the need for good sense or for looking ahead and taking responsibility for the likely consequence of our action or inaction. However, such belief has an impact on good sense. For example, it does, or should, make us willing to take bold action when this is what God seems to be calling

> Providence is the care and foresight by which God provides for the world and humanity so that things are able to achieve their end.

us to do. It also helps us to avoid the temptation to make ethical compromises under threat of bad consequences. If we do what is right then we can leave it to God to sort out the consequences. To return to the teaching of Jesus, if we seek the kingdom of God; that is, if we seek to do what is right and to follow the promptings of the Spirit, then we need not be anxious about what the future holds.

That everyone has a guardian angel appointed by God is an expression of God's particular care for each person.

God is not only the Creator of all things, but is the Creator of each of us, knows each of us intimately, and has a plan for each of us. The theological virtue of hope gives us a consciousness of personal providence that transforms the way we experience the world. It does not remove our everyday hopes or fears but it inspires us to relate all our hopes and fears to God in prayer (as will be explored in a later chapter), and it liberates us from our deepest fears. It is the recognition that my life is in the hands of God.

Love & friendship with God

There are different ways to understand the moral life. Some people think the essence of morality is a law (by which actions are forbidden, permitted, or required). Others think that morality should be thought of as a set of duties recognised by the person (perhaps the most famous proponent of this view was Immanuel Kant). Others start not with duties but with rights, like the Universal Declaration of Human Rights adopted by the United Nations in 1948. Aristotle, as we have seen, began not with laws, duties, or rights but with the virtues or excellences that make someone a good person.

Christianity contains each of these elements. It accepts the enduring validity of the moral law given to Moses and especially the Ten Commandments. It accepts also that people who do not have any religion can do right and avoid wrong because of a law written on their hearts (Romans 2:15). This is commonly termed the 'natural law'. 'Natural' here just means belonging to human beings because of what we are and what fulfils our nature, rather than being revealed by God (as is the Divine law) or written by society (as is the civil law). The natural law includes duties towards others which can also be understood in terms of the rights of others. Finally, while Christians may differ from Aristotle in some of the character traits they see as virtues, Christianity certainly gives emphasis to the roots of action in the dispositions of the heart.

Moral action can reasonably be thought of in relation to laws, duties, rights or virtues. However, as argued in the first part of this book, the most fundamental meaning or measure of the moral life is not in laws or even in virtues but is in relationship between friends.

The theological virtue of love or charity is that gift of God that enables us to love God with the love of true friendship and to love others as God loves us.

Section 2

The importance of friendship in life gives reason for becoming a good person, for if we wish to have a good friend we need to be a good friend. There are obligations we have to strangers, not to harm them or unduly restrict their freedom, but if we are not open to becoming a friend with someone and do not share a common life with him or her then we will remain alien to one another. The meaning of life, and hence of morality, is that kind of love we call friendship.

The Last Supper

We learn about friendship from our relationships with one another as we grow up together and make, break and occasionally rediscover relationships of love. The theological virtue of love or charity is that gift of God that enables us to love God with the love of true friendship and to love others as God loves us. This love inspires in us the desire to serve God, the desire to serve those who God loves (especially the poor) and the desire to enjoy the company of God for ever. The claim of Christianity is that all our friendships are only possible because of a love that existed before we were born, before even the Universe existed: the love of God. This is what the poet Dante (d. 1321) called 'The Love which moves the sun and the other stars' (*Divine Comedy, Paradiso*, Canto XXXIII, lines 145). Even more amazingly, according to Jesus, his disciples will not only be valued servants of God but will actually become friends with God, 'No longer do I call you servants, for the servant does not know what his master is doing; but I have called you friends, for all that I have heard from my Father I have made known to you' (John 15:15).

'The Love which moves the sun and the other stars' *Divine Comedy, Paradiso*, Dante

Christian education, then, is not only about coming to know something (knowledge) or coming to know how to do something (skill), or even about becoming a certain kind of person (virtue); it is about coming to know someone. *Christian* education is above all a process of growing in friendship with God in Christ.

'No longer do I call you servants, for the servant does not know what his master is doing; but I have called you friends, for all that I have heard from my Father I have made known to you' John 15:15

On the face of it there is something scandalous, even absurd, in the claim that human beings could enjoy friendship with God, for friendship is characteristically an equal and mutual relationship, whereas there is no more unequal relationship than that between creature and Creator. There is nothing that the Creator needs from the creature nor anything the creature has that he or she did not receive from the Creator. Even the achievements of human efforts are themselves the work of the Creator.

Aristotle in his account of friendship states that true friendship is only possible among equals. In relationships that are unequal – the relationship of teacher and student, of doctor and patient, of master and servant, for example – it is generally regarded as unprofessional, dangerous, or unfair for the person in the stronger position to seek friendship from the relationship. These relationships can be positive, respectful, rewarding, but they are by their nature unequal and so they are endangered if the vulnerability of the weaker party is not acknowledged. This is part of the reason why boundaries are needed to maintain good professional relationships.

Analogously, it seems very dangerous for human beings to call themselves friends of God. Thinking of myself as a friend of God and in some sense equal to God could easily make me proud, and pride, as we have seen, is the most dangerous of the vices. On the other hand, to think of God as my friend could lead to me bringing God down to my level: having a tame and comfortable idea of God. This would not be the true God, the awesome and terrible Creator of the entire universe, but would simply be an 'imaginary friend'. The language of friendship with God is therefore potentially dangerous because it could lead Christians to have a proud and unreal view of themselves, or a small and unreal view of God, or both.

The idea that the Christian life is a life of friendship with God is therefore something that we should think of as paradoxical and not to be taken for granted. Nevertheless, it is at the very heart of Christianity. It is God, in the Incarnation, who has united our nature to his own. So also, the deepest meaning of 'grace' is not just the free action of God. The deepest meaning of grace is the personal presence of God the Holy Spirit in our hearts and it is the Holy Spirit who establishes in us a relationship of friendship with God. Human persons are not equal to God by nature but we can become 'divinised' in a certain sense by the gift of the Holy Spirit within us. We can be friends with God because God gives this friendship. Another way to say this is that, in Christ, God has become one with us and we are granted a share in the inheritance of Christ, his Divine Son and our Divine and human brother. We have been made children of our heavenly Father, not by nature, but by adoption.

'Love God and do as you please'. St Augustine

There are different ways to understand the moral life and there is something to be said for many of these accounts. Acting well does imply keeping the commandments, respecting the rights of others, cultivating the virtues, and promoting the Common Good. However, from the Christian perspective these aspects are secondary to the first meaning of the good life which is friendship, and most fundamentally friendship with God. In the words of Pope Francis, 'Christian morality is not a form of stoicism, or self-denial, or merely a practical philosophy or a catalogue of sins and faults. Before all else, the Gospel invites us to respond to the God of love who saves us, to see God in others and to go forth from ourselves to seek the good of others. Under no circumstance can this invitation be obscured! All of the virtues are at the service of this response of love' (*Evangelii Gaudium* 39). From love and the requirements of friendship all else follows. This is the meaning of the seemingly rash advice of Augustine, 'Love God and do as you please'.

6. Christianity & the Task of Education

Some pointers for making use of this chapter

This chapter includes discussion of the idea of secularism and modern attempts to suppress religion. It directly addresses concerns raised about whether faith schools are necessarily divisive or whether they have a legitimate place in modern secular society. This theme, and the themes of selection, inclusivity and elitism are particularly relevant to governors, and may be useful material for induction of new governors and training or reflection days for governors, where these are provided. These topics could also provide interesting and perhaps provocative material for discussion among staff.

Curriculum links

OCR

G571: AS Philosophy of Religion (Religion and Science)

AQA

AS Unit H Religion and Contemporary Society (RSS08) (Faith schools, secularism)

A2 Unit 3F Religion and Contemporary Society (RST3F) (Faith schools, secularism)

A reasonable case for the teaching of religion

As the gospel reshapes our understanding of the virtues, so it provides a new perspective from which to understand education. Historically this perspective has been the inspiration for the foundation of schools and universities and for generations of Christian teachers. However, before considering what is distinctive in a Christian approach to education, and how this can and should shape the ethos of a Church school, it is necessary to address an objection to the very idea of Catholic education.

The gospel provides a new perspective from which to understand education.

It has been argued that, at least within the state-funded system, education should always be based on secular principles and should never be based on any particular religion. Organisations such as the National Secular Society object not only to the teaching of religion from a Christian perspective but also to the very existence of Church schools. Such schools are permitted to apply religious criteria in the admission of pupils and in the employment of staff. Secularists argue that such admission and employment practices are discriminatory, restricting the choices of nonreligious parents and the employment opportunities of nonreligious teachers. They also claim that such schools pose a threat to community cohesion.

In addressing these objections it is useful to start by asking whether, from a naturalistic or secular perspective, religion should be among the range of subjects that students study at school. A healthy understanding of human flourishing will include body, mind, and spirit. Religion addresses fundamental questions that human beings have always asked and continue to ask: Why am I here? What should be my aim in life? Does my life have any meaning in relation to the world? Does the world itself have a personal meaning and a transcendent origin? Are there forces of good and evil in human history that are more than the sum of human decisions? How should we face death? What happens to the life of a human person after his or her death?

Historically speaking, religious belief is not the exception. It is the norm.

It is true that these questions could be answered without any reference to religion. These fundamental questions are the subject of *philosophy* and have been considered by many great thinkers who were not conventionally religious, from Plato to the present day. Nevertheless, for most people in most periods of history answering such questions has not been either a purely philosophical or a solitary activity. Most people's thinking about life and death and God and the world has been shaped and supported by the practice of a religion. If we look at the great sweep of history we can see that religion is practised to a greater or lesser extent in every period of time and in every part of the world. Historically speaking, religious belief is not the exception. It is the norm.

Even if there is only one possible unified theory, it is just a set of rules and equations. What is it that breathes fire into the equations and makes a universe for them to describe? Stephen Hawking: *A Brief History of Time*

Stephen Hawking

As the body seeks healthy activity and the mind seeks knowledge so the human spirit seeks meaning. If there is a source of all meaning, all being, life and reason, then human rational creatures will find their meaning in relation to this ultimate source of meaning. The virtue of religion is the disposition of a rational creature to acknowledge and honour the Creator. Particular religions are visible communities with particular traditions of practice (words and rituals) by which adherents seek to show honour to God. Christianity is a religion in this sense. In general monotheistic religions (such as Judaism, Christianity and Islam) seek to makes sense of human life and death, human joy and suffering, in relation to the One God who transcends the whole world, and on whom the whole world and each individual creature depends for our life and existence. Religion can of course go bad, as all good things can go bad, but in itself finding meaning through religion can be seen to be a significant part of human flourishing. Even an atheist, who believes that there are no gods and that religion is based on an illusion, will appreciate the importance of knowing whether or not there is a source of meaning that transcends the world. Some atheists, indeed, have argued passionately that it is of the greatest importance to establish that there are no gods, in order to be free from religion and free to face the world honestly as it really is. In this sense atheism is also a kind of religious belief (that is, a belief about religion) and has its own rationale for studying religion.

There is, therefore, a good 'natural' case to be made that a complete education should include religion, both in the generic sense of religion as the human search for ultimate meaning and in the sense of studying religions. Nevertheless, in the last two hundred years or so (since the Enlightenment), Western societies have grown increasingly uneasy with education practised within or according to a specific religious tradition. It is often pointed out that religion historically has been the occasion (if not the cause) of much conflict. This is also obvious in the present day, not least in the Holy Land. People of different religions disagree and sometimes those disagreements turn violent. So philosophers such as Immanuel Kant argued that society should discourage the emotional and irrational elements in religion and that religious education should be restricted to what can be known 'within the limits of reason alone'.

> The virtue of religion is the disposition of a rational creature to acknowledge and honour the Creator.

Theology: Suppression of Religion

It is undoubtedly the case that terrible things have been done in the name of religion. On the other hand, attempts to suppress religion in the name of 'Reason' or 'Science', whether in the French revolution or in communist Russia, have involved violence and intolerance at least as bad as that caused by religion. It is for this reason that G. K. Chesterton (d. 1936) argued that, precisely because religious and philosophical ideas can be so dangerous, it is necessary to be familiar with them and to understand them: 'Religious and philosophical beliefs are, indeed, as dangerous as fire, and nothing can take from them that beauty of danger. But there is only one way of really guarding ourselves against the excessive danger of them, and that is to be steeped in philosophy and soaked in religion' *Heretics* ch. XIV.

Secularism & religious diversity

Education reflects society and is ordered towards the good of society, and modern Western society is secular, at least in the sense of aspiring to be open to full participation by those of all religions and none. For this reason it has seemed to many people that formal education should be secular rather than religious. On this view, it would be arbitrary or unfair for a school to give priority to one religion, such as Christianity, rather than studying all religions and treating them all as equal. The problem with this view is that actual religion (as opposed to religion in the abstract) is always *a particular religion*. The idea that we should 'stand back' from all religions would effectively mean that we should not commit ourselves to any particular religious opinion or identify ourselves with any particular religious community. This is unfair to all religions and gives preference to the uncommitted or to those positively committed to atheism. It may indeed be the case that some atheists wish to establish schools that are based on such a philosophy, but there is no *a priori* reason that this perspective should be preferred in general, let alone required of all schools. Indeed, if religion, at its best, is a form of human flourishing, then this is surely understood better by those who practise a specific religion, whatever that religion is. A Hindu may not have a perfect understanding of Christianity but a Hindu, Muslim or Jewish perspective on Christianity will tend to capture more than a detached nonreligious view of Christianity.

Indifferentism seems a fair and respectful approach to religion, but in fact it is very patronising.

A related idea is that, to be fair about religions, one should say that all religions are the same. This is not generally the same as atheism, which is the view that all religions are false. However, it is 'indifferentism' (the view that no one philosophy or religion is better than any other) or 'syncretism' (the attempt to fuse different religions or philosophies into one). Indifferentism seems a fair and respectful approach to religion, but in fact it is very patronising. Rather than listening to what different religious traditions say, and properly acknowledging their differences, it asserts that the differences cannot be important, or that people do not understand their own traditions. There are of course many important truths that different religions hold in common, but to respect religious diversity is precisely to acknowledge that there are differences, as well as similarities. Similarly, syncretism involves the creation of another philosophy or religion and is not the abolition of differences between religions, just as Esperanto was the creation of a new language not the abolition of differences between languages. Indeed, because there will be many ways to select and combine different elements of different religions, there will be many different forms of syncretism. Of any one of these it can be asked: why should we believe this rather than that, live in this way rather than that way?

In politics, ethics, and other important matters, some opinions will in fact be better than others - more truthful, more adequate, more helpful - but people also have to live with ongoing disagreements about what is the best way to think and to act. People have to learn to live together at the same time as coming to some view on what is right or good or honourable, and promoting this view in their social and political activities. The same is true of religion. There are different religions and they are not all the same or all as good as one another, but until the time that everyone embraces one single religion, people also have to learn to co-exist - particularly in our own, highly diverse society - while holding on to what they believe is good and true. This is the basis of a different understanding of secularism. Secularism when it becomes an ideology, what is sometimes called 'programmatic secularism', involves suppressing all expression of religion in the public sphere and thus effectively imposes a form of state atheism on all citizens.

Secularism when it becomes an ideology, what is sometimes called 'programmatic secularism', involves suppressing all expression of religion in the public sphere and thus effectively imposes a form of state atheism on all citizens. In contrast an older and more tolerant form of 'procedural secularism' allows access to the public sphere to those of all faiths and none and thus protects free speech and conscience both for individuals and institutions.

Section 2

In contrast an older and more tolerant form of 'procedural secularism' allows access to the public sphere to those of all faiths and none and thus protects free speech and conscience both for individuals and institutions.

Myth: education can & should be 'neutral' about religion

It is a myth that the only fair approach to religious education is 'neutrality' between all religions and none - teaching *about* religions but not teaching from any religious perspective. This myth appeals to a fictitious 'view from nowhere'. It is like the idea that people from different parts of Britain have 'regional accents' but that people from the South East of England speak without an accent. In fact everyone has an accent and it is just that one accent (in England, a form of middle class Southern English) happens to be dominant. There is no way to speak 'neutrally', without an accent. A tolerant form of secularism will not impose agnosticism on everyone but will allow different communities to teach about religion from their own perspective. A tolerant secularism will encourage religious communities to teach their own tradition and to find, from their own resources, ways to promote peace among people of different religions.

A pluralistic secularism should accept that people find meaning within different particular religious traditions and will allow different communities to express their belief and to teach it to their children. This indeed is one of the fundamental rights of parents. The whole basis of secularism is to embody the virtue of tolerance in the public sphere in relation to religion. This will include, for example, allowing communities to teach that marriage consists in a lifelong committed relationship between one man and one woman. The definition of marriage is not primarily a religious issue, but it is an example where prohibiting expression of a more traditional view would involve suppressing religious freedom.

Ecumenism

This is not to say, however, that just anything counts as a religion or that there are no limits to tolerance. Tolerance is a virtue and thus a mean between opposite vices (bigotry and indifference). Religion, like all human goods, can contain bad elements and can go bad; indeed, there are sects that are harmful both to their adherents and to the Common Good. How then can one distinguish healthy, or at least tolerable, religious diversity from the distortion of religion represented by cults such as scientology (not to mention the complete inversion of religion in devil-worship)? Jesus said 'by their fruits you shall know them' (Matthew 7:16) and this is a good rule of thumb. Over time, well-established religions have shown their fruits through their contribution to human life and society through healthcare, education, art and culture and in many other ways. This can be said to a greater or lesser extent of all the great religious traditions and most certainly of Christianity (as will be argued in more depth in the last part of this book). Christianity provided the very foundation for school and university education in Europe. To suppress specifically Christian schools, as some organisations seek to do, would not only be an illiberal denial of tolerance; it would be an act of ingratitude, and a denial of our own history (that is, of the history of the Western world).

Why Christianity requires a new understanding of education

There is a good case, then, for teaching religion, and particularly within the United Kingdom for permitting the teaching of Christianity and supporting Church schools. But what does Christianity actually add to the vision of education set out in the first part of this book? If education aims at developing the mind and at the integral formation of the human person, then how can Christianity add anything substantial to this aim? Of course Christianity has an important role in providing a particular community and a particular tradition which give us a place and a sense of history through which to learn about being human. It gives sources for teaching about right and wrong: for example, the Ten Commandments (Exodus 20:1-17 and Deuteronomy 5:6-21) as well as wise advice (for example, in the books of Proverbs and Ecclesiastes). It gives us the example of Jesus, and of the saints – those Christians who lived heroic, pure and virtuous lives. If the Christian contribution to education were understood in this way then, while Christianity would add specific content, it would not radically change our view of the world. It would simply provide extra help and advice for living the kind of life that a good pagan like Aristotle or Cicero would recognise as honourable and desirable. It would not need its own philosophy of education or its own distinctive ethos.

There is, however, a problem with thinking of Christian education primarily in terms of moral rules, good advice, and the good example of Jesus and the saints. The account of Jesus given above, and the Christian account of the virtues this implies, demonstrates that Christianity radically alters our understanding of human flourishing and of how it is to be pursued. Jesus did not just reveal what it is to be a good person; he also made some very specific claims about himself, about his heavenly Father, and about the Holy Spirit. Furthermore, in what happened to him, Jesus revealed a deep problem with the way human beings are now. Jesus lived a good life. He taught with authority and gave people hope and meaning. He also cured people of their diseases and reconciled people who had been excluded from the community. He fed crowds with miraculous food and even raised the dead. And yet despite doing these wonderful things, Jesus was tortured to death. In fact he was killed precisely because of his good actions, because he was perceived as a threat to the status quo. His death was not an act of violence inflicted randomly or by someone on the fringe of society. He was killed with the full approval of secular and religious leaders of his day. His death was the culmination of the actions and inactions of many seemingly good, respectable people.

The crucifixion of Jesus shows there is something deeply wrong with the world, a tendency to sin that is found even within the most respected and most well-educated members of society. This poses fundamental problems for the natural account of

Section 2

education set out in the first part of this book. Children have natural curiosity and are attracted to the goods of knowledge, skill, and friendship, and education aims to introduce students to, and prepare them for, participation in a wider world of culture and activity. However, that very world of culture is deeply flawed. There are the obvious flaws of gross inequality, criminal behaviour, and the shallow cult of celebrity. Furthermore, the most respectable elements of society have deep failings that are even now being exposed. Recent scandals have hit our democratic parliament, our independent press, our police and judiciary, our health service, even the priesthood and religious communities. Nor is it only a matter of schools or families shielding children from the 'outside world', for schools and families are part of the world and have their own flaws.

There is a problem with thinking of Christian education primarily in terms of moral rules, good advice, and the good example of Jesus and the saints.

Processes are therefore put in place to protect children from children, and children from teachers, and teachers from children, and teachers from teachers. Even the family may need to be supported by social services. These institutions represent a serious attempt to keep children from harm and, in the most extreme cases can even take children from their parents for their protection. However, we know that sometimes the signs are there but that a child is not saved in time, and sometimes a child is removed from danger only to come to harm in a care home or in a foster family. So also, sometimes a child is wrongly removed from his or her parents so that both the child and the parents suffer terribly. There is no human institution that is free from the problems of human error and human vice. The question is often: Who guards the guards? How can we educate children in the virtues of society when society itself is so much in need of reform?

Since it is easy to see the faults in society, and to some extent the faults in ourselves, people have sometimes thought that, if only children were protected from culture, and allowed to act simply according to their natural instincts, then they could naturally acquire virtue. This is the romantic ideal of an innocent state of nature. However, while education does (or should) build on natural curiosity and the best learning is active learning, it remains the case that all education, however carefully mediated, is an introduction to the human world of culture. The word 'culture' comes from cultivation of the soil but has come to mean the development of mind and especially its artistic and intellectual development and the human achievements that have followed from this. 'Man comes to a true and full humanity only through culture' (*The Church in the Modern World* § 53). There is no way to join this world without being shaped by it.

> The word 'culture' comes from cultivation of the soil but has come to mean the development of mind and especially its artistic and intellectual development and the human achievements that have followed from this.

The idea that human virtue is to be attained by seeking a state of pure nature, (without the corrupting effect of society), is sometimes attributed to the philosopher Jean-Jacques Rousseau (d. 1778). However, Rousseau was well aware that a child cannot flourish or acquire the virtues without education, and that education requires a tutor. In fact children are positively harmed when they are neglected and left too much to their own devices. The dark possibilities of this kind of situation are explored in the novel *Lord of the Flies*. This is fiction, but is credible because of the well-known effects that can result from lack of supervision and lack of good adult role models. This is what we should expect, given the doctrine of original sin. It is not only the adult world that can be cruel.

Criteria for success & criteria for selection

Christianity therefore demands a new account of education, one that acknowledges the weakness of the present human condition and our need for God's grace. However, before setting out what might be involved in such an account, it is useful to examine some attempts at resisting this conclusion. Even among Christians there can be a more or less explicit desire to keep hold of the respectable, tidy, classical account of human virtue and its implied account of education.

In the early Church this attitude was exemplified by the British ascetic Pelagius (d. 420). He thought that if we did not stress hard work then Christians might return to their old bad habits and then make excuses. For Pelagius there were no excuses. God has given a law to tell people what to do and each person has the ability to follow it so that no one has any excuse for doing the wrong thing. Moral education, on this view, consists simply in teaching the moral law and requiring students to put it into practice. Pelagius was himself morally very serious. He advocated and kept to a strict discipline of avoiding indulgence. This seemed to many people a reasonable and indeed admirable approach to Christianity. However, Augustine immediately recognised that this attitude contradicts the core of the Christian message in that, by denying original sin, it denies our radical and continual need for God's grace. In reality, even our turning to ask for God's help can only happen because of the action of God within us.

There is an ever present danger that Christian education can fall into Pelagianism. This is precisely what happens when sin and grace are forgotten and Jesus is presented simply as a good example: as a role model for teachers and students. Christianity can then be seen as a system in which hard work is rewarded by success and in which those who succeed, whether academically, in sport, or in their future career, are the authors of their own success. This is all the greater danger if a school is successful in the conventional sense, as Church schools often are. It is a problem not only because it can lead to distorted priorities and superficial standards of success, but more deeply because it is not founded first on gratitude and a recognition of our continual dependence on others and on God. There is a Christian virtue of aspiring to great things (magnanimity or large-heartedness),

St Augustine of Hippo

but this, as we have noted, is shown in service of others. Christianity acknowledges the extent of human failure and is directed, most characteristically, to helping those in most need. Christianity can indeed be applied to the task of educating the elite of society and those who are destined for worldly success, but it is more characteristically expressed in the education of those who are marginalised, poor, socially deprived, or who have special educational needs.

There is an ever present danger that Christian education can fall into Pelagianism.

There is a danger, then, that a school, despite being Christian, will adopt criteria of success that imitate too closely the criteria of success in wider society, and forget not only the broader sense of human flourishing, but also the hope that is founded not on past success but on grace. A related danger is that a school may seek success by unreasonably excluding children who are unlikely to succeed in a worldly sense, or who need extra support to do so. This danger also finds an echo in the controversies of the early Church.

Theology: Elitism in the early Church

During a time of persecution some priests and bishops renounced the faith and then, when the persecution came to an end, they asked to return and were reconciled. This action of accepting people back who had publicly betrayed the faith was shocking and scandalous to many Christians in North Africa who had suffered terribly under persecution. Most Christians in North Africa came to belong to a breakaway church led by a bishop called Donatus (d. 355). They refused to be in communion with any church that permitted the reconciliation of those who had betrayed the faith. However, other Christians in North Africa remained in communion with the rest of the Church throughout the world. To show they belonged to the universal Church, these Christians called themselves 'Catholics'. Augustine was Catholic bishop of Hippo in North Africa. He was Catholic in that he belonged to the universal Church in communion with Rome.

Augustine had to remind his fellow Christians of a parable that Jesus had told precisely against this tendency to elitism and separation. Jesus spoke of a man who found that an enemy had sown weeds in his grain field. The man tells his servants not to uproot the weeds, or they would uproot the wheat at the same time. They should wait until harvest time and only then separate out the weeds and the wheat (Matthew 13:24-30). In this parable the harvest time is the final judgement and the field is the world where weeds and wheat grow up together. The Church herself is a mixed body and any attempt to purify the Church by permanently and completely excluding people will do harm and will contradict the words of Jesus. Any exclusion from the community must be partial, reversible, and should aim to benefit the person temporarily excluded.

It was argued above that it is entirely reasonable for a Catholic school to give priority to Catholic pupils, for these schools were founded to support Catholic parents in the education of their children. Attempts to require a Catholic school to turn Catholic pupils away in favour of a certain quota of non-Catholic pupils are an expression of an illiberal form of secularism, an attack on the Catholic community. Nevertheless, precisely from a Catholic perspective it may be problematic or at least regrettable if pupils are selected on the basis of how regular their parents are in the practice of the faith. In many dioceses, if a Catholic school is over-subscribed, the local bishop may allow the school to prioritise 'practising Catholics', meaning those who strive to observe the Church's requirement that they attend Mass on Sundays and Holy Days of Obligation. This reflects the importance of parents as the primary educators of the child and may be a reasonable compromise where there is not sufficient provision for all Catholic children. Nevertheless, the Church has a duty to all those who, by baptism, are true members of the Church and who have not renounced it, even if their parents are not regular in their practice. Such admission policies therefore beg the question of what provision is made for the religious educational needs of these other Catholic children. More problematic still are policies that go beyond a simple definition of 'practising Catholic' and that reward the level of commitment, as measured by various parish activities. It needs to be asked whether such practices are compatible with the Catholic character of the school.

Attempts to require a Catholic school to turn Catholic pupils away in favour of a certain quota of non-Catholic pupils are an expression of an illiberal form of secularism.

The issue of academic selection by examination is not straightforward. It might or might not be reasonable depending on what provision other Catholic schools are making for those of less academic ability. This is equally true of covert forms of selection which aim to improve the reputation of a school by choosing pupils who are more likely to be successful. Different children have different aptitudes and it is not the individual school but the Catholic school system as a whole that should aspire to have places available for all Catholic children. Nevertheless, if the system as a whole should make such provision this will, of necessity, involve some schools making provision, for example, for Catholic children who have behavioural problems or who have special needs or who lack strong parental support or who for other reasons are unlikely to achieve academic success. Within the sector schools may specialise, and some will choose to educate those of greater academic ability. However, the mark of the Catholic community as *Catholic* will be the provision it makes for the education of all its members, and in particular for those within the community whose need is greatest and those who are marginalised. A Catholic school should thus reflect a different understanding of success and a different set of priorities for admission than those found in wider society.

A grace-haunted account of education

It is perhaps useful to reiterate at this point that a Catholic account of the aims and virtues of school education will embrace many elements that are also accepted by non-Christians. These will include, among other things, the development of the mind, the fostering of human freedom, the integral formation of the human person, the primacy of learning over teaching, and the primary role of the parents in education. The Church also recognises the importance of education for the transmission of culture and the economic benefits of education to pupils and to society. A school is designed 'not only to develop with special care the intellectual faculties but also to form the ability to judge rightly, to hand on the cultural legacy of previous generations, to foster a sense of values, to prepare for professional life'. Nevertheless, it should also be clear from the above discussion of Jesus and of the Christian virtues that Christianity does not so much add discrete elements to this account of education as transform it radically, not only in relation to the ultimate aim of education but also in regard to the way that aim is pursued.

The unity of the human person as body and soul is hugely important in thinking about ethics.

The image of education presented by Aristotle is one of slow and patient improvement, by practice under the watchful care of an expert tutor. It is a well-ordered process in which results are expected and success builds on success. In contrast, the image of education presented in the gospel is of a complete change of heart, dramatic and unexpected. After meeting Jesus, people were converted and their lives were transformed. People had felt trapped, dead inside, without hope, and after meeting Jesus they found forgiveness and a new life and new hope. This change of heart did not build on their past success but it rescued them from past failure.

Aristotle thought that it was simply not possible to be a good and virtuous adult if you had a bad start in life: a deprived or a spoilt upbringing. It was simply too late. He thought that for some people there was no hope of ever attaining true happiness. True human flourishing was only for the privileged, the elite, and was not even possible for women, or anyone who had to work for a living! In contrast Christianity from the first has been a message of hope for all people and of transformation of lives, whatever our background. In educational terms this does not mean abandoning the nurturing of good habits: the concept of virtue remains indispensable. However, it does mean recognising and making allowance for the brokenness that is all around in society and that may be present even in a child, and taking seriously the grace that can bring a new start at any stage in life, and can surprise the teacher as well as the one taught.

Education: The importance of understanding Original Sin for education

Pope Pius XI in his 1929 encyclical on education warned that 'every method of education founded, wholly or in part, on the denial or forgetfulness of original sin and of grace, and relying on the sole powers of human nature, is unsound'. In comparison with what we might call a natural view of education, the doctrines of original sin and Divine grace make Christianity both more pessimistic and more optimistic. It is more pessimistic in that it admits that the problems of the world go very deep, even to the heart of things, and that no one is immune from their effects: not even teachers, not even children. This means that a Christian school must provide pastoral support for staff and for children at times when they are not seeing success. The Scriptures present God as careful to sustain life and hope when it is most vulnerable, 'the bruised reed he will not break, and a dimly burning wick he will not quench' (Isaiah 42:3). On the other hand Christianity is at the same time more optimistic because it writes no-one off but sees the possibility of a new start and a new life for everyone. This is not based on visible strengths, past success, or privileged opportunities, but relies on the power of God that comes from outside and is now at work in the world.

Rev Dr Rowan Williams

A gradual growth in power and confidence, of the kind Aristotle advocated, is thus not the only possibility; Christianity acknowledges that people's actual lives are often untidy and full of ups and downs. Indeed, Christianity sees education as making progress often precisely through this untidiness: through weakness and failure as well as strength and success, though spontaneity as well as planned activity, by accident (that is, by providence) as well as by pedagogical design. As Pope Francis reminds us, 'God's word is unpredictable in its power. The Gospel speaks of a seed which, once sown, grows by itself, even as the farmer sleeps (Mark 4:26-29). The Church has to accept this unruly freedom of the word, which accomplishes what it wills in ways that surpass our calculations and ways of thinking.' (*Evangelii Gaudium* 22). This has implications for the anxious over-planning and over-activity that is a feature of much modern education. Rowan Williams captures this well when he writes, 'the believer's vision ought to be such as to be hospitable to the idea that effects are, in a grace-haunted world, unpredictable and disproportionate to effort. A school or other institution perpetually panicking about its timetable is communicating very effectively a model of human living inimical to religious faith in general and to Christian belief in particular' (*Education! Education! Education!*, page 172).

An account of education that is 'grace-haunted' will have relevance not only to religious education classes but will, or should, touch every subject area and the ethos of the school as a whole.

An account of education that is 'grace-haunted' will have relevance not only to religious education classes but will, or should, touch every subject area and the ethos of the school as a whole. This was recognised clearly by Pius XI who argued that, to

Section 2

be a fit place for Catholic students, 'it is necessary that all the teaching and the whole organization of the school, and its teachers, syllabus and text-books in every branch, be regulated by the Christian spirit, under the direction and maternal supervision of the Church; so that Religion may be in very truth the foundation and crown of the youth's entire training.' This implies that a Christian view of education will require not only Christian teachers but Christian institutions, that is, Church schools. The final section of this book will therefore consider education in the context of a Catholic school. It will start with a reflection on the impact of Christianity on culture, as this is the context within which Christian schools and universities were first founded and such reflection also helps to show how a Christian vision sheds light on diverse subjects across the curriculum.

3. The Church & Education,
What should a Catholic School look like?

7. A Light to the World

Some pointers for making use of this chapter

This chapter includes reflection on a variety of different subjects in relation to the contribution that Christianity has made to the progress and self-understanding of each. It also addresses the myth of the alleged cultural conflict between Science and Religion. This material may be useful, especially in conjunction with material from the previous chapter, to demonstrate the value of Christian approaches to education and thus of Church schools. In addition to possible use during induction of new staff or governors this chapter could help provide a focus for cross-curricula activities such as Christian Unity Week. The chapter could be used to inform heads of each department to plan a lesson appropriate for each year group in Christian Unity Week, so all pupils would be informed and have an opportunity to discuss the effects of Christian influence in 'lighting-up' the educational world, and helping to shape the disciplines taught in schools. There could also be a role for chaplaincy in leading on this week and helping to make apparent the links between subject teaching, religious assemblies, and the aim or ethos of the school.

Curriculum links

OCR

OCR G571: AS Philosophy of Religion (Science and Religion)

AQA RS

AQA RS AS Unit C Philosophy of Religion (RSS03) (Religion and the Modern World)

AQA RS AS Unit D Religion, Philosophy and Science (RSS04)

AQA RS AS Unit E either The History of Christianity or Religion, Art and the Media (RSS05)

AQA RS AS Unit H Religion and Contemporary Society (RSS08)

AQA RS A2 Unit 3 Studies in Religion (RST3A, RST3C, RST3F) (Science and Technology, Contemporary Society)

AQA RS A2 Unit 4 Religion and Human Experience (RST4B, RST4C) (Contemporary Society, Visual Arts)

AQA Philosophy

AQA Philosophy Unit 3 PHIL3 Key Themes in Philosophy (Reason and Faith)

AQA Philosophy Unit 2 PHIL2 An Introduction to Philosophy 2 (The Value of Art)

Edexcel

Unit 2 Area A: The Study of Religion (Science and Religion, Creative expressions of Religious Life)

Unit 2 Area E: The Study of the Old Testament/Jewish Bible (Religion and Science)

Unit 2 Area F: The Study of the New Testament (Religion and Science)

The impact of Christianity on culture

In general what we achieve, even when it is by our own efforts, is only possible because of the debt we owe to others - because of what others have done before us. There is no such thing as a self-made man any more than there could be a woman who gave birth to herself. We were born of others, and others reared us, and we have not only a particular debt to our parents, but also to our culture, for the language through which we engage with and understand the world. This debt is particularly obvious in the world of education, research and scholarship. The teacher will bring something of her own understanding to the task of encouraging students to think and sharing with them the knowledge and skills of her subject, but the whole task of education presupposes something already there to pass on, a body of knowledge, a way of understanding the world. Formal education also presupposes a system of schools, universities, teacher training and a society that encourages and supports (more or less) the great task of educating the next generation. The teacher may also have a particular debt to people who taught or inspired her, at school or university.

These are general truths, and they should not be controversial. We owe a debt to those who have gone before, who have passed on and enriched our culture. With a little reflection it should be clear that, in the same way, contemporary Western culture, and in particular the world of learning and education, is deeply indebted to Christianity. This is obvious in the case of Church schools and subjects such as religious education, but the same is in fact true in some way of all schools and of all subjects.

Christianity has contributed to schooling and to learning in at least three ways:

First, by the commitment to preserving and passing on knowledge. This is seen vividly in the preservation by monasteries of writings of the ancient world, even of pagan poets and philosophers, at a time when the Roman empire had collapsed and the 'secular' world was in disarray during the 'Dark Ages'.

A Canticle for Leibowitz

It was recognition of the contribution of the monasteries to the preservation of knowledge over centuries that inspired one of the great science fiction novels of the twentieth century, Walter J Miller's *A Canticle for Leibowitz* (1960). Deeply affected by his involvement in the bombing of the ancient monastery of Monte Cassino during the Second World War, Miller wrote of a future in which nuclear war leads to a new dark ages and it is again only the monasteries that keep alive what learning remains. The imaginative power of the book comes from its attempt to portray a thousand years of future history and the contribution to that history of a single continuous institution. Miller invites his readers to see afresh the extraordinary achievement of those institutions that did endure for more than a millennium from the decline of the Roman empire to the rebirth of Europe in the high Middle Ages and the Renaissance, during which time, and indeed up to the present, they have been engaged continually in the work of education.

It is also seen in the founding of Catholic schools, and in the founding of hospitals and universities, including the ancient universities of Bologna, Paris and Oxford. As well as founding many health and educational institutions, the Church continues to sustain them: It has been estimated that in 2012 the Catholic Church in America alone spent over 115 billion dollars on health, schools and universities. (*The Economist* 16 August 2012)

Lemaître and Einstein

Secondly, by the way the message of Christianity contains elements that have encouraged the study of different subjects, the development of different disciplines, not only in general but in particular, as will be discussed further below.

Thirdly by the contribution of particular Christian individuals or institutions to their disciplines: of Isaac Newton to physics, of Gregor Mendel to genetics, of Mgr Georges Lemaître to cosmology. This third contribution, of which many examples are given below, could be dismissed as accidental, as though these scientists' Christianity had as little to do with their achievements as the fact that Newton was English, Mendel Austrian, or Lemaître Belgian. They had to be from somewhere and they will have had some attitude to religion. Why should it be of any significance that they happened to be Christian? The answer to this is twofold. In the first place it mattered *to them* that they were Christian: they understood their scientific work as an aspect of their faith. In the second place because certain Christian doctrines had given them courage, for example, to look for a deeper order to things, or to understand the world as a cosmos – as a coherent whole. This twofold significance shows how a worldview can influence both the motivation for and content of learning.

Section 3

This chapter will trace some of the ways in which Christianity, and in particular Catholic Christianity, has had an impact on the different disciplines. It is not only of interest in itself but it is also helpful, at a time when the very existence of Church schools is in question, to recall the role of Christianity in shaping the foundations of education in Western countries. It may also help those working in a Catholic school to understand how the work of the whole school, across the curriculum, relates to a Christian worldview - this is a topic to which we will also return.

The modern world is immensely indebted to the intellectual culture fostered by Christianity. However, as emphasised in the second section of this book, Christianity does not portray a world in which one would expect uniform and inevitable progress. The message of the gospel is one of hope, but it is a hope that is based on acknowledging past and present sins, within as well as outside the visible Church.

The Christian gospel would thus lead us to expect an ambivalent story, in which the Church's substantial contribution to learning and education would nevertheless be hampered by human vices and by the misuse of the claims or institutions of Christianity as an excuse or an opportunity to exploit others. For example, Christianity is a missionary religion. It is this that inspires its efforts to explore every place and learn every language and learn about every culture. This inspiration has led to the founding of schools and hospitals around the world, to educational opportunities, especially for the poor who had no access to education, and it has sometimes led to the challenging of unjust or cruel practices such as the exposure of infants or the burning of widows. On the other hand the spread of Christianity has often been interwoven with the empire building of European countries, the violence of the conquistadors, and the greed of trading companies - even the trading in human beings.

In the same way we should not be surprised that the progress of knowledge and culture, in general promoted by Christianity, has sometimes been hampered by Christians: sometimes by zealots, for example, those who destroyed icons or stained glass windows, or who encouraged paintings to be burned on a 'bonfire of the vanities', or who were afraid of new knowledge; sometimes by worldly compromised Christians, by those who had little concern for the care of the sick or the education of the poor, or who placed short term or personal political gain over the good of society and only supported the search for knowledge when it had immediate pragmatic objectives. If Christianity gives us an accurate picture of the world, this uneven and inconstant progress is what we would expect.

The heavens declare the glory of God (the natural sciences)

An aspect of Christianity which undoubtedly encouraged study of the natural sciences is its doctrine of creation: that the world is not the result of random or accidental forces but is the work of a Creator and therefore a well-ordered whole. Pope Francis writes that faith 'illumines the material world, trusts its inherent order and knows that it calls us to an ever widening path of harmony and understanding.' At the same time faith 'encourages the scientist to remain constantly open to reality in all its inexhaustible richness. Faith awakens the critical sense by preventing research from being satisfied with its own formulae and helps it to realize that nature is always greater' (*Lumen Fidei* 34). To explore the universe is to explore God's handiwork, a spiritual motivation that is denied to those who view science purely as a means to material benefits. This also allows Christianity to value knowledge for its *own sake* and not only as a way of achieving control of nature and of the world through political, military or economic power. The word 'science' simply means knowledge but since the nineteenth century has been reserved for the natural sciences. The natural sciences (that is the physical and the life sciences) employ various forms of observation, experiment, and mathematical analysis in order to attain precise and characteristically quantitative knowledge of physical reality. Since the seventeenth century these disciplines have grown exponentially in their power to understand physical reality, from below the microscopic level to the limits of the astronomical.

The natural sciences (that is the physical and the life sciences) employ various forms of observation, experiment, and mathematical analysis in order to attain precise and characteristically quantitative knowledge of physical reality.

Among all the sciences, it is perhaps physics, astronomy, and cosmology that have most attracted believing Christians. This is seen as early as the work of the Franciscan friar at Oxford, Roger Bacon (d. 1294), on the nature of light. This early work is notable for its emphasis on empirical, experimental methods and the role of mathematics in understanding the physical world. Light is a metaphor for spiritual understanding, and for the very life of God, but it is also an aspect of the beauty of the world, a world created 'in measure, number and weight' (Wisdom 11:21, a favourite quotation of many early Christian writers). Shortly after Bacon's work, the first spectacles were invented in Italy, while Cardinal Nicholas of Cusa (d. 1464) is believed to have been the first to discover the benefits of concave lenses for the treatment of short-sightedness. Such innovations were driven both by the desire to alleviate suffering and by a desire to understand the created world.

It was with the invention of the telescope that a great era of astronomy emerged in the sixteenth century, where Christians were able to apply the words of the psalm and 'look at your heavens' (Psalm 8:3). A key figure in this revolution was the Catholic cleric Nicolaus Copernicus (d. 1543), who proposed heliocentrism, according to which the earth and planets orbit the sun, as an elegant mathematical model of the universe. His work was built on by a later generation of observational astronomers and mathematical physicists, on both sides of the Catholic-Protestant divide: Galileo Galilei, Johannes Keplar, Tycho Brahe and perhaps the greatest of all physicists, Isaac Newton. Without exception these thinkers conceived their work as theological in inspiration.

Nikolaus Kopernikus

At this time Galileo Galilei (d. 1642) courted controversy not only by the claims he made but also by the way he argued for them. He was unwilling to confine himself to defending heliocentrism only as a mathematical hypothesis, but neither did he have the physical proof he needed to overturn accepted interpretations of natural philosophy and of the Scriptures. He also made the mistake of appearing to ridicule Pope Urban VIII, who was in fact one of his supporters. Famously his case came before the Roman Inquisition, he was forced to recant, and his works advocating heliocentrism were censored. Nevertheless, within the context of those turbulent times Galileo was treated with relative leniency. He lived first as a guest of the Archbishop of Siena, and, while confined to his villa, he carried on writing, seeking in vain for the demonstration that always eluded him. It should also be noted that even at the time of the Galileo trial there were Jesuits teaching heliocentricism in Rome using the detailed observations of the Protestant astronomer Tycho Brahe.

Galileo would not have understood his case as a conflict between 'science' and 'religion' (both of which are nineteenth century terms). He saw himself as a loyal Catholic offering a scientifically rigorous interpretation of the Scriptures. He thought that the Church had taken too uncritically the claims of previous (Aristotelian) natural philosophers. It should also be noticed that his unwillingness to treat heliocentrism as a purely mathematical model stemmed from his conviction that the order observable by astronomers is a real feature of the created world - created by God and not just created by human minds. In his own day, Galileo had no way to prove this conviction and it was only a much later generation of cosmologists who were able to devise methods for determining the movement of earth and sun relative to other stars. Nevertheless, Galileo shows how a Christian worldview supports 'scientific realism' and challenges scientists to continue to strive to *prove* their hypotheses.

Perhaps the most dramatic Catholic contribution to cosmology was the hypothesis of cosmologist Fr Georges Lemaître (d. 1966) that the world began as a primitive atom which exploded in what critics dismissively termed the 'big bang'. This theory is now as central to cosmology as evolution is to biology. It is striking that while Fr Lemaître was honoured by the Pope, who appointed him to the Pontifical Academy of Sciences (1936), he was vilified by atheists who attacked his theory specifically because it conflicted with their ideology. In the Soviet Union opposition to 'big Bang' theory, along with Mendelian genetics - also attacked because discovered by a Catholic cleric, and because unknown to Karl Marx - continued until the 1960s. Scientists who defended these theories risked not only their reputations but their freedom and their very life. Some of these scientists, such as Nikolai Vavilov (d. 1943), died in Soviet concentration camps.

Myth: The warfare of Science & Religion

It is thus a myth that through history religion has impeded the progress of science and medicine. The classic statement of this myth is found in A.D. White's book *The Warfare of Science with Theology in Christendom* (1896). White devotes an entire chapter to the allegedly malign effects of religion on medical progress. This chapter is worth examining because it remains influential. Not only is it available in its entirety on the internet but examples from this chapter have been reiterated in public debate up to the present day. One example may suffice to give a flavour of the argument.

'In 1847, James Young Simpson, a Scotch physician, who afterward rose to the highest eminence in his profession, having advocated the use of anaesthetics in obstetrical cases, was immediately met by a storm of opposition... From pulpit after pulpit Simpson's use of chloroform was denounced as impious and contrary to Holy Writ; texts were cited abundantly, the ordinary declaration being that to use chloroform was "to avoid one part of the primeval curse on woman."'

This example has been much quoted. However, the evidence for this 'storm of opposition' is limited to a pamphlet written by Simpson, a Christian, in which he defends his practice against real or imagined critics. In fact no Christian denomination, no Christian tract, no prominent Churchman opposed the development of anaesthetics. The idea of significant Christian opposition to anaesthetics in childbirth seems to be a myth based on a Christian tract *defending* the innovation. Since the 1960s it has been widely recognised that the thesis of a generic and repeated 'conflict' of science and religion is inadequate to the historical data. It ignores the debt which medicine and science have to earlier generations of Christian scholars and scientists. It is a classic case of *eisegesis*, historians reading into texts and events a significance that these did not carry in their original context.

In regard to the study and ordering of living things, monastic orders played a key role in the Middle Ages in developing and applying learning to agriculture. One of the great polymaths of the middle ages was Albert the Great, teacher of Thomas Aquinas, who was perhaps the next great observational biologist after Aristotle. Whereas Thomas was a philosopher and theologian delighting in thinking through arguments to their conclusions, Albert went in search of minerals and vegetables, quizzed midwives, gamekeepers and falconers, observed the behaviour of animals (and which parts were edible – he does not recommend the beaver's tail!)

The key theory of modern biology is evolution, developed brilliantly by Charles Darwin who, despite his Christian upbringing, became doubtful of the existence of God. However it should also be remembered that it was Jean-Baptiste Lamarck (d. 1829), a French Catholic, who first developed a theory of evolution of species and the evolutionary genealogical tree. It was not in fact Darwin but his friend T.H. Huxley who associated Darwinism with a stridently atheistic worldview, while Darwin's cousin Francis Galton applied his theory to the elimination of disabled people for the sake of what was termed 'eugenics' or 'racial hygiene'. These developments are not necessary consequences of Darwin's theory but examples of how scientific theory can sometimes be misunderstood philosophically or can get mired in political ideology.

Section 3

The Catholic Church, while it condemned racist theories of human origins and similar forms of 'social Darwinism' never forbade evolution from being taught in Catholic schools or universities. It was a problem for some Christians who are biblical literalists but the Catholic Church and the Catholic school system which was well developed in the nineteenth and early twentieth century never encountered a problem with the teaching of evolution. To give clarity for Catholics, in the 1950 encyclical *Humani Generis* the Church confirmed that there are no intrinsic conflicts between Christianity and theories of evolution, provided that the scientific theory does not claim to determine that human beings have no spiritual life or that spiritual souls are generated by a material process.

Spreading the word (languages & literature)

Christianity is intimately associated with language and literacy. This is because words can express truth that is of Divine origin, including the words of the Jewish Scriptures (the Old Testament) and the sacred writings of the first Christians (the New Testament).

'the same things uttered in Hebrew, and translated into another tongue, have not the same force in them'. Prologue to the book of Sirach

Pentecost in the Upper Room

For any religion which has a sacred text, people will be concerned about the precise meaning of each word, and so will tend to be suspicious of translation, for no translation can be perfect. Indeed, in the prologue to the book of Sirach (in Catholic Bibles) the translator, who is the grandson of the author, apologises because 'the same things uttered in Hebrew, and translated into another tongue, have not the same force in them'. However, in some ways the work of translation is essential to Christianity. Judaism is the religion of one specific people with its own history. It needs only one language. Other religions seek to spread one particular culture to all nations and so need only the language of that culture. Christianity, in contrast, is a gospel that is intended for every nation and culture. This is shown for example in the miracle of Pentecost when the Holy Spirit came upon the disciples of Jesus who started speaking in different languages so those who heard them asked, 'And how is it that we hear, each of us in his own native language?' (Acts 2:8)

'And how is it that we hear, each of us in his own native language?' Acts 2:8

The command of Jesus to go and proclaim the message of the gospel to all nations requires that the message is translated into a language that will be understood. It is also important that, as stated above, within Christianity the most perfect revelation of God is found not in the sacred words of the Old or New Testaments, but in the very person of Jesus, 'the Word made flesh'. The words on the sacred page find their meaning in relation to a living human being, Jesus Christ, and they can be translated because they are spoken and heard within a living community, inspired by the Holy Spirit.

As an example of the sacrifices made to overcome language barriers, Jerome (d. 420) spent twenty-three years writing an accurate Latin translation of Scripture (the Vulgate) from Greek and Hebrew. While Latin is the language of many religious texts and much beautiful Church music, it should be remembered that Jerome was working on a vernacular translation, making the text accessible to people who could not read Greek or Hebrew.

In the same way throughout the centuries missionaries have translated works into the language of the people. Sometimes the Bible has been among the first of works to be written down and has helped maintain or defend a language and a culture. Thus the translation of the Bible also helped create or set alphabetic systems, as it did with the Cyrillic alphabet, now the principal alphabet of Slavonic languages such as Russian. Even when writing was well established, a particular translation of the Bible has sometimes been expressive of a culture at a particular time and remains a valuable part of the literary culture, as with the King James Version of the Bible in English or Luther's translation of the Bible into German.

The significance of Latin for Western Christianity is not what Arabic is for Muslims or Hebrew for Jews: it is not the unique language of the Word (for the Word has been made flesh and is now encountered by speakers of many languages). Nevertheless, Latin is a doorway both to the deeper understanding of the unity underlying many modern European languages and a doorway to the tradition of the Church, her thought, her prayers and her music.

For most people, the wish to learn a language is not connected to a wish to speak about religion. However, a Christian understanding of language can help show how, at its most general, learning a language and speaking a language is about learning about others, about their culture and way of life. It is not the linking of words in dictionaries but an invitation to a human encounter; this of course includes an encounter with people who have gone before and thus with ancient languages.

The word literature simply means what is written, and in this sense everything from a letter to a shopping list is literature. In a world that is full of writing and where texts multiply with every passing moment, this raises the question: what makes some words more worthy of our attention - more worth reading? We give the name 'literature' especially to narratives or well-crafted phrases which express well some significant human meaning. The word 'poem' simply means something 'made' but, again, this word is used for a particularly well-made literary passage (or one which attempts to be such). Literature

We give the name 'literature' especially to narratives or well-crafted phrases which express well some significant human meaning.

is characteristically about people: human words about human beings. It may be the author speaking directly about his or her own life. The genre of the autobiography was perhaps invented by the early Christian bishop Augustine of Hippo. The *Confessions* is an account of his own life and how he understands this as a discovery about himself.

Augustine was ambivalent about the literature and plays of his day, and was critical of himself for having shed tears over fictional characters while not paying sufficient attention to the needs of real people. Another reason for his ambivalence was the focus of this literature on worldly matters, on human emotions and on distorted ideals of honour, rather than on God or on eternal truths. Nevertheless, within Augustine's Christian worldview there was a role for the 'worldly' as the place of our pilgrimage through life. The worldly city and the City of God are intertwined until the world ends, as it will one day. According to this vision, literature might be expected to express an ambivalence: seemingly focused on the immediate and the human rather than the sacred (in the sense of the churchy), it may nevertheless disclose meaning that is ultimately sacred.

This sacred meaning is easy to see in the literature of the Middle Ages in the *Divine Comedy* of Dante Alighieri, in William Langland, and in Geoffrey Chaucer and is evident, for those who see it, in the plays of William Shakespeare. However, even in the Middle Ages and the early modern period, poets and playwrights wrote vulgar bawdy comedies as well as poems about refined ideals, and wrote of human love as well as divine love. The modern genre of the novel, rooted in medieval romances, is frequently the vehicle for light entertainment, for predictable stories of romance, crime or action that are an escape from reality rather than a guide to it. However, well written fiction in any genre reflects and discloses human emotions, human actions and human meaning and this is of Christian significance precisely because everything human, when it is not trivialised, is of Christian significance.

A number of twentieth century Catholic novelists, including Francois Mauriac, Graham Greene, Evelyn Waugh, Flannery O'Connor, and Shusaku Endo, have explored ideas of religious meaning in the midst of human failure including seeming religious failure. They do not portray Christianity as a moral law that everyone follows or a road that is easy. They show the gospel rather as a revelation of human need and a hope that exists despite apparent failure. In this way they reflect a Catholic vision that is close to that of Augustine and far from the kind of smug moralistic attitude exemplified by Pelagius which is a perennial danger for Christians. There are also Christian poets who have written on explicitly religious themes, such as John Milton, Gerard Manley Hopkins, and T.S. Eliot, but more fundamentally there is a Christian way to approach all poetry and indeed all literature. Whatever discloses the human, discloses the Divine.

Theology: Contrasting approaches to Christianity & literature

A contrast in the different approaches to Christian literature may be found by comparing C.S. Lewis with J.R.R. Tolkein. Both wrote fantasy novels that helped establish the genres, but whereas those of Lewis contain very explicit Christian allegory, Tolkien, who was a devout Catholic, preferred to explore Christian themes more indirectly. *The Lord of the Rings* trilogy is not a disguised retelling of the gospel story, but is a tale shot through with Divine providence and many other themes of Christian thought, such as victory over evil coming through fidelity, love and sacrifice rather than physical strength. It shows the possibility of corruption and of redemption, and most characteristic of all, it shows victory coming through apparent weakness.

To the ends of the earth (history & geography)

The word 'history' is linked to the idea of a narrative or story. Christianity is not only the revelation of a timeless truth, but is a story of salvation. In Judaism, the Scriptures are understood as five books of the law and then further books of prophecy and history that illustrate that law. In contrast, Christians tend to read the whole of the Old Testament as a story that culminates with the coming of Christ. Of course the Old Testament includes law and prophecy and many other kinds of writing, but what gives unity to the Old Testament as a whole is the great story of the human race and, within this, of the Jewish people, from whom would come a saviour of all nations. The most important writings in the Christian Scriptures are the Gospels, which are four narrative accounts of the life, death and resurrection of Jesus. Even the Apostle's Creed, that touchstone of Christian belief, is really a compact narrative: of creation, the birth, death and resurrection of Christ and the hope of his second coming and the life of the world to come.

In common with other religions which have a cycle of festivals, the Church has given great attention to accurate dating of the seasons. In particular, the fixing of the date for the liturgy of Easter (on the first Sunday after the full moon after the northern hemisphere's vernal equinox), was a strong incentive to develop an accurate, universal calendar. In the sixteenth century Luigi Lilio and the Jesuit Fr Christopher Clavius were the main architects of the Gregorian Calendar (1582), named after Pope Gregory XIII and now the principal calendar of the world. The unique event of the birth of Christ is, for Christians, a turning point dividing the whole of history into BC (before Christ) and AD (in the year of the Lord) and provides a way to date years other than by reference to kings or empires (the typical dating system in the ancient world). The spread of Christianity has enabled this system to provide a common reference for dating events so that even those historians who are not believers can see the benefit of dating events as occurring in the common era (CE) or before the common era (BCE).

Section 3

'there is nothing new under the sun' Ecclesiastes 1:10

Many ancient societies regarded time as cyclical, repeating eternally like the cycles of the stars. From this fatalistic perspective, 'there is nothing new under the sun' (Ecclesiastes 1:10). By contrast, as Fr Jaki (d. 2009) argued, the incarnation breaks this dreary circle. So for Christianity time is *linear*. This understanding underpins the notion of historical progress: a valuable notion, even though it has been distorted by Whig historians and by Marxists to mean inevitable improvement.

In addition to these principles, the early Church considered her own historical continuity to be a vital sign of authenticity, as shown in records of the apostolic succession of bishops. In the late second century, for example, Irenaeus listed the bishops of Rome in unbroken succession from the time of Peter and Paul (*Against Heresies*, III.3). The succession of bishops of Rome, the papacy, remains the oldest continuous political institution in human history and, as with any human institution, has built up archives and museums that are a treasure-trove for historians. In a similar way at a local level, records from parishes and monasteries are invaluable for studying the history, the economics, and even the climate of previous ages.

There are books of history in the Old Testament, and there were chronicles and histories in the ancient world before Christianity. Nevertheless, while Christians did not invent history they have practised it from the time of the *Ecclesiastical History* of Eusebius of Ceasarea (d. 339) and the *Ecclesiastical History of the English People* of Bede the Venerable (d. 738), down to the present day. Nor have Christians only been concerned with Church history or the history of Christian institutions, for, from a Christian perspective, there is no history which does not disclose humanity and no history that is outside the providence of God.

'go into all the world' Mark 16:15

If Christianity has encouraged and enriched the study of history, even more so has it promoted interest in geography: physical and human. Christ's commission to the Church to 'go into all the world' (Mark 16:15) and to 'teach and baptise all nations' (Matthew 28:19) required missionaries to leave familiar people and places and explore all the regions of the world. The first Christians were Greek-speaking Jews within the Roman Empire, but the faith soon spread from Jewish to Gentile converts, from Greek to Latin speakers and then beyond the limits of the Roman Empire, which at that time was the limit of the known world, to the Celts, Saxons, Indians, Slavs and so on. To do this required explorers and encouraged map making. For such reasons, Christian cultures have consistently encouraged the exploration of the world, though the explorers and their political and commercial sponsors have also had other motives, not least financial.

'teach and baptise all nations' Matthew 28:19

Setting out from Catholic Europe in the high Middle Ages, Marco Polo (d. 1324) explored Asia on a journey that took twenty-four years and covered 15,000 miles. The great Age of Exploration began with the Portuguese Prince Henry the Navigator (d. 1460) who organised a series of voyages down the west coast of Africa. Subsequent explorers included Bartolomeu Dias, who rounded the southern tip of Africa (1488), Columbus, who sailed the Atlantic and found the Americas (1492) and Magellan's expedition of 1519–1522, which included the first crossing of the Pacific and the first circumnavigation of the globe. These achievements should not be regarded as simply due to technological developments in ships, clocks, or navigational instruments; rather, it was the desire to explore that drove the technology.

Bartoleme de Las Casas

With the age of discovery came colonialism and forms of exploitation of which Christians were critics and, sometimes, apologists. Neither empire building nor slavery began with Christianity; indeed, the movement to abolish slavery from the world has largely been Christian in origin. While the slave owners appealed to the 'real world' of capitalism, and sometimes to Aristotle and sometimes to the imagined superiority of certain races, opponents such as the Dominican friar Bartoleme de Las Casas (d. 1566) or the English Protestant William Wilberforce (d. 1833) were driven by a Christian concern for the dignity of each and every person made in the image of God. Nevertheless, while the prophetic voice of these Christian critics would eventually win the day, many Christians and Christian institutions went along with their country and their class and allowed Christianity to be used as a cloak for nationalism, exploitation and slavery.

In the late twentieth century, the era of post colonialism, Christians have taken a lead in working for development and international justice. This is seen in the number of aid agencies that are or originally were predominantly Christian, and also in the actions of the Vatican (for example the letter of Paul VI in 1967 *Populorum Progressio*) and other Christian bodies in seeking to bring issues of international justice to the attention of the more powerful nations of the world. There have also been economists who have sought to criticize the very foundations of their discipline and find an alternative basis in an account of human flourishing. Such accounts are closely parallel to the natural account of the good of education set out in the first part of this book. One notable example of this is E. F. Schumacher (d. 1977), who wrote *Small is Beautiful* and was subsequently led to embrace Catholicism. Christians have sometimes been criticized as naïve about economic realities of trade, capital and production, but the credit crunch and world economic downturn of the early twenty-first century have shown that enthusiastic free market capitalists can also be open to the charge of naivety.

Beauty so ancient and so new (art and music)

The word 'art' at its broadest refers to the skill of making something well so that it is useful and/or beautiful. Christianity has had such a close association with art over the centuries that it would be extremely difficult to imagine the development of the Western canon without the Church's involvement. In ancient Judaism, people were forbidden from making images (Exodus 20) so that they would not worship idols as they had worshiped the golden calf (Exodus 32). A similar fear of idolatry seems

The word 'art' at its broadest refers to the skill of making something well so that it is useful and/or beautiful.

Section 3

to lie behind the aversion to representational art in the history of Islam. Indeed, fear of idolatry has even driven some Christians, including certain Byzantine emperors in the eighth century (the 'iconoclast' dispute) and some Protestant Reformers in the sixteenth century (such as the Puritans in England) to destroy much religious art.

John of Damascus in the eighth century wrote, 'I boldly draw an image of the invisible God, not as invisible, but as having become visible for our sakes by partaking of flesh and blood'. On the Divine Images, First Apology.

The reason why Catholic and Orthodox Christianity have taken a different stance is rooted ultimately in the Incarnation. John of Damascus in the eighth century wrote, 'I boldly draw an image of the invisible God, not as invisible, but as having become visible for our sakes by partaking of flesh and blood' (On the Divine Images, First Apology). Just as the fear of idolatry led to an aversion to all representative art, the belief that Jesus is God made visible has made all representational art potentially holy. This position was officially confirmed by the Second Council of Nicaea (787) in an edict that supported the subsequent development of representational art in the Catholic and Orthodox world.

Madonna and Christ Child

As far as we know, Christian art may well be as old as Christianity itself. What is certain is that there was a flourishing of mosaics, stone carvings and painting after the legalisation of the public expression of Christianity in the fourth century. The use of the word 'icon' for an image of Christ or a saint dates from at least the fifth century. According to Bede in his *Ecclesiastical History*, when Augustine (of Canterbury, to be distinguished from Augustine of Hippo who lived in Africa two hundred years earlier) landed in England in 597 he arrived with a large processional crucifix and icons, bringing art as well as faith.

In the Middle Ages stained glass windows, statues and wall paintings were an important part of sharing the faith with people who could not read. Some modern opponents of Christianity criticise the time and money spent on building and ornamenting medieval chapels and cathedrals, but it should also be remembered that this art was accessible to the masses. The idea of public art had to be reinvented in a later age with art galleries and museums, but in its original context religious art was nearly always public art. It was a witness to a shared belief, a means of communicating the faith, and at the same time a way in which ordinary people could share in the appreciation of beauty. For all created beauty is a reflection of the transcendent Beauty that is God.

The tradition of religious art saw great developments in technique, so that Giotto (d. 1337) is credited with initiating a new realism in painting, developing techniques of drawing accurately from life, using perspective devices and expressing emotions through his depictions of the human face. Brunelleschi (d. 1446) is credited with inventing one-point linear perspective in painting, with Alberti (d. 1472) explaining the mathematical theory. The work of Fra Angelico (d. 1455), today the patron saint of art, expressed theological insights, especially those of Thomas Aquinas, using the new methods of the High Renaissance.

The sixteenth century saw an extraordinary flowering of religious art especially but not only in Italy and in Ghent. At this period there was also a marked increase in domestic art: portraits, landscapes and still lives painted for the homes of an expanding upper-middle class. The nineteenth century witnessed the creation of many different styles of painting and a greater divergence of religious and secular painting. For the first time for centuries, the Christian religion ceased to be the principal patron and subject of the arts, while culture increasingly embodied a romantic conception of the artist as a heroic individual expressing his or her unique inspiration rather than a practitioner of a craft or a tradition. In the twentieth century art has become further fragmented between, for example, commercial art, used to ornament or sell things, 'high art' in galleries and the lobbies of businesses, and what one might call folk art: representational art made for pleasure or sold for a modest fee.

Afghan girls: Every portrait is an exploration of the human

In this fragmented world religious themes have sufficient cultural resonance that they can still be invoked in great works of public art such as Antony Gormley's Angel of the North. Moreover, as well as the more explicit references and the historical contribution of Christian artists to technique and to the shared cultural imagination, it is also possible to understand all art (all making or imagining) in a Christian sense. Every portrait is an exploration of the human (just as much as literature), every landscape an exploration of creation (just as much as the natural sciences), and every act of making an exploration of form and beauty (or sometimes, an exploration of the breaking down of human meaning).

'And I heard a voice from heaven like the sound of many waters and like the sound of loud thunder; the voice I heard was like the sound of harpers playing on their harps, and they sing a new song before the throne' Revelation 14:2-3

In relation to music, there is a similar pattern. Music is intimately connected with Christian prayers and ritual. According to Augustine, the Christian who sings 'prays twice': once in the words and once in the beauty of the music. The Scriptures even associate music with the vision of heaven, 'And I heard a voice from heaven like the sound of many waters and like the sound of loud thunder; the voice I heard was like the sound of harpers playing on their harps, and they sing a new song before the throne' (Revelation 14:2-3).

Section 3

From the early Middle Ages, Christian civilisation has contributed to the development of the Western musical tradition. Drawing on Jewish antecedents, especially the psalms, in its early liturgical music, this musical style crystallised from the sixth century into 'Gregorian chant'. The name of this monophonic music comes from Pope Gregory the Great (d. 604) who promoted its use in Europe's monasteries. It was in a monastic context that notation was developed for recording chant on parchment. These techniques led to the invention of modern musical notation (staff notation) and also to the 'ut-re-mi' (do-re-mi) mnemonic device (invented by Guido of Arezzo, d. 1003).

Around the turn of the first millennium, Europe's Cathedral schools developed early forms of polyphonic music which harmonised and alternated voices in chant. The *Winchester Troper* (c. 1000) is the oldest extant example of notated polyphony. In the fourteenth century, De Machaut (d. 1377) composed the *Messe de Notre Dame* for Rheims cathedral, creating the first polyphonic Mass that is sometimes credited as the first known instance of a unified extended musical composition by one person. Some Catholic and Protestant church leaders were suspicious of polyphony, because the music could make it hard to hear the words of the liturgy. Despite this, the genre remained popular, and composers such as Palestrina (d. 1594), Tallis (d. 1585) and Byrd (d. 1623) received royal and ecclesiastical patronage. The pinnacle of the complexity of the genre is exemplified by Tallis's *Spem in Alium* which is for forty voices. While this form of music has but one instrument (the human voice) the complex harmony of many different parts anticipates the orchestral music of a later age.

Gospel Choir Singers

Another explicitly religious musical genre is the oratorio, literally a 'prayer', developed as an extended piece of music. Famous oratorios include Handel's *Messiah* and *The Dream of Gerontius*, a poem by John Henry Newman set to music by the Catholic composer Elgar (d. 1934). Such interplay of religion and music moves easily across confessional borders. J. S. Bach (d. 1750) wrote music for Lutheran liturgies that borrowed many elements from the Mass. The forms of the liturgy, and Church patronage, also shaped and enabled many works by Monteverdi (d. 1643), Vivaldi (d. 1741), Mozart (d. 1791) and Beethoven (d. 1827). Among many more recent works, the great *Symphony No. 8* of Mahler (d. 1911) takes as its principal theme the ancient hymn of Pentecost, Veni creator spiritus, while Dvorak's *Symphony to the New World* draws on spirituals – the Christian hymns of black slaves.

Although hymns are often associated with the Reformation (both in England and in Germany), vernacular hymns were already popular in the Middle Ages. Many popular hymns in England date back to the nineteenth century where there was a flourishing culture of hymn writing among Catholics, Anglicans and Methodists, with popular hymns used by all of the denominations despite their suspicion of one another.

While hymns are religious, they are designed to be popular, with a simple and memorable melody so that they can be sung without musical notation. They draw on and remind us of the popular folk culture that runs in parallel to 'high culture' (whether religious or secular). Modern means of recording and sharing music have created a pop-music industry that is without parallel in earlier generations, but for as long as there has been music there have been popular forms of music for dancing, drinking-songs, and ballads telling of love, or of tragedy or, sometimes, of politics.

The association of some forms of music with dancing, drinking and disorderly (and sometimes harmful) behaviour have made Christians in different ages, including our own, cautious about some forms of music. Certainly some lyrics and some subcultures seem to condone or romanticise violent or otherwise irresponsible behaviour, so as to make such caution fully justified. Nonetheless, there remains a place for youthful exuberance and also for exploring independence and this also is an aspect of human life which is God-given. The role of the school may well include engaging with the forms of music that students listen to, or at least analogous popular and accessible forms, through which to introduce key musical ideas.

Musical education should provide the opportunity to expand the appreciation of musical forms precisely in order to understand the many ways that music can speak to the human person. To reiterate a theme that has run through this chapter, as well as music (whether in high or in popular culture) that has an explicit religious theme, there is a Christian way to understand music *as such*. What discloses the human discloses the Divine, and the appreciation of music discloses something profoundly human. Music can express human emotions and be apprehended by human reason. It seems to be something we join, which shapes our sympathies to align with those with whom we share the experience (Scruton, *Understanding Music*, p. 54). It is possible to make music on one's own, but music is typically a way in which people are together, and together engage in and with something mysterious, a meaning that is encountered but cannot be articulated adequately in language.

8. The Ethos of a Catholic School

Some pointers for making use of this chapter

This chapter provides a clear history of Catholic education and may be helpful for schools in relating their own history and character (for example as a former Salesian school or as a recent academy) to the larger history of Catholic education. It is not a substitute for a school's awareness of its own institutional history, but it provides a context within which to understand that particular story. It also provides a useful starting point for anyone wishing to look at the key Vatican documents on education.

The understanding of the Catholic school as a communion is a central concept of the theology of Catholic education and should be the core of regular INSET and induction prior to discussion of the practicalities of curriculum and policies. The Catholic school as communion would also make an appropriate staff/governor retreat theme.

The section on prayer is of particular relevance to chaplaincy, and strongly affirms its role in seeking to establish that the rhythms of the Church be reflected in school days, weeks and the whole academic year, through time-tabled prayer. The great challenge is in supporting all staff to engage in this.

Curriculum links

AQA

RS AS Unit H Religion and Contemporary Society (RSS08) (Faith schools, secularism)

RS AS Unit K World Religions 2: Christianity (Prayer)

RS A2 Unit 3F Religion and Contemporary Society (RST3F) (Faith schools, secularism)

RS A2 Unit 3H World Religions 2: Christianity (Christian spirituality, prayer, communities)

Edexcel

Unit 2 Area B: The Study of Philosophy of Religion (Prayer)

Unit 2 Area D: The Study of World Religions (Religious practice in a multicultural society)

The impact of Christianity on education

As Christianity has contributed to, and helped to shape, each of the disciplines taught in school, so it has contributed to the discipline of teaching itself. Indeed it is difficult to overestimate the contribution of Christianity to the understanding and practice of education. For much of the history of Western Europe, the Church was virtually the sole provider of formal education, and even when secular educational institutions began to emerge in the nineteenth century, they remained indebted to the insights and accomplishments of generations of Christian educators.

For much of the history of Western Europe, the Church was virtually the sole provider of formal education.

King's School, Canterbury

After the fall of Rome, and the collapse of many areas of social and cultural life, it was the Catholic Church, and in particular the monasteries, that preserved a literary culture within Western Europe. These institutions functioned as centres for education and founded schools, often associated with cathedrals. A good example is the oldest school in England, King's School in Canterbury founded in 597.

St Augustine's Abbey

In the twelfth and thirteenth centuries, the monastic and cathedral schools gave way to new educational institutions, with their own independence, the universities. The word *universitas* described a specialized association of students and teachers with the status, in law, of corporate personality. By the middle of the fifteenth century there were already over fifty universities in Europe supporting study in a range of subjects. They had liberal arts faculties as well as theology faculties, and not only trained clerics in sacred theology but typically also taught law and medicine and an increasing variety of particular disciplines. Nevertheless, while they were not attached to a particular monastery or bishop, and were not only for theological studies, the universities were self-consciously Christian institutions. Many of these universities, such as Oxford, still show signs of their Catholic foundation, not least in their architecture and numerous chapels. However, it was only in the nineteenth century, when the original vision of a Catholic university was being contested, that it received perhaps its clearest articulation with John Henry Newman's *The Idea of a University*.

At the same time that higher education was being established, the Church also made efforts to extend provision of education more broadly, especially to the poor. The third Lateran Council in 1179 decreed that every cathedral church make funds available for

Section 3

someone to teach the clerics of the cathedral and 'poor children who cannot be helped by the support of their parents' (canon 18). The Council decreed that, in addition to cathedrals, other churches and monasteries that had formerly provided such a teacher should restore the practice. Also, in an effort to remove obstacles to the expansion of teaching, it forbade churches from making money by selling a licence to teach. It was common practice in parishes for priests to teach locally, acting as tutors to children whose families could pay and providing free or subsidised teaching to poor children. Nevertheless, while the Church provided certain educational opportunities for the poor, in a predominantly agricultural economy where children worked from an early age, relatively few parents sought out formal education for their children.

The Reformation saw the destruction of many monasteries and religious houses which had provided education, but also saw the founding of many schools, colleges, and universities. Within Protestant communities there was a drive for greater literacy spurred on by the priority given to private reading of the Scriptures. This emphasis also encouraged the study of the biblical languages and work on new translations of the Scriptures. At the same time, within the Catholic community, there was a renewal movement associated with the Council of Trent (1545-1563) and with the founding of new religious orders, most notably the Society of Jesus (the Jesuits). These new religious movements were not monastic or unworldly, in that they did not require a regular communal life or advocate withdrawal from the world. Rather, they were missionary and humanistic. They sought to bring the gospel message to the world and to recognise the work of God in the world. In 1548 the Jesuits founded their first school in Messina in Sicily, not as a seminary for the training of priests but to provide a general humanities education to Catholic young men. By the late eighteenth century the Jesuits were running over 800 schools and universities.

The Salesians of Don Bosco are now among the largest religious orders and run more than 2000 schools and colleges.

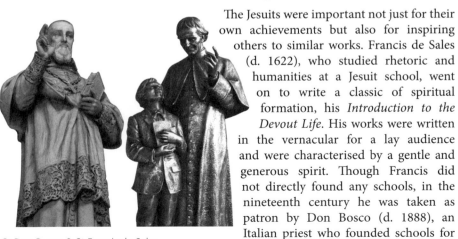

The Jesuits were important not just for their own achievements but also for inspiring others to similar works. Francis de Sales (d. 1622), who studied rhetoric and humanities at a Jesuit school, went on to write a classic of spiritual formation, his *Introduction to the Devout Life*. His works were written in the vernacular for a lay audience and were characterised by a gentle and generous spirit. Though Francis did not directly found any schools, in the nineteenth century he was taken as patron by Don Bosco (d. 1888), an Italian priest who founded schools for

St Don Bosco & St Francis de Sales

the poor. Don Bosco developed an approach to education which he called 'preventive' in which experience of the love of God and his providence 'comes before' (*prae-venire*) human actions. He developed this system as an alternative to educational approaches of his day which he perceived to be based on threats and punishments. He described his system as 'based entirely on reason, religion, and above all on loving-kindness'. The Salesians of Don Bosco are now among the largest religious orders and run more than 2000 schools and colleges.

The eighteenth and nineteenth century saw the founding of many religious orders devoted to teaching. These included many orders of religious sisters who promoted the education of girls. The twentieth century saw further contributions to educational theory by Catholics; for example the system developed by the Italian doctor Maria Montessori (d. 1952), which emphasises the interactive and developmental character of learning. It was also a Catholic, Shinichi Suzuki (d. 1998), who developed the pioneering method for learning the violin based on nurture rather than on nature. In the twentieth century there was a remarkable increase in the number of Catholic schools so that currently there are approximately a quarter of a million Catholic schools educating approximately fifty million students. It is also the case that an increasing proportion of Catholic schools are now run partly or entirely by lay people, that is, by teachers who are neither priests nor members of a religious order. This trend has seen a number of schools moving from religious orders to lay control. In the context of such expansion and change, the Second Vatican Council produced a document on education and in 1967, the Congregation for Catholic Education was restructured to give more support to Catholic schools (not only to seminaries and Catholic universities). The Congregation has produced a number of formative documents beginning with *The Catholic School* in 1977.

Key documents produced by the Congregation for Catholic Education

1977	The Catholic School
1982	Lay Catholics in Schools: Witnesses to Faith
1988	The Religious Dimension of Education in a Catholic School
1997	The Catholic School on the Threshold of the Third Millennium
2002	Consecrated Persons and their Mission in Schools
2007	Educating Together in Catholic Schools (A shared mission between consecrated persons and the lay faithful)
2009	Letter to the presidents of bishops' conferences on religious education in schools
2013	Educating to Intercultural Dialogue in Catholic Schools: Living in Harmony for a Civilization of Love
2014	Educating Today and Tomorrow: A renewing passion (*Instrumentum laboris*)

It is noteworthy that as this history has unfolded, older patterns have not entirely disappeared but have either been incorporated into new forms or continued alongside them. Some of the oldest Christian schools still exist, while the pattern of monastic

Section 3

schooling is represented by contemporary Benedictine schools. Similarly Jesuit schools co-exist with Salesian schools and these co-exist with newer lay-run schools. It would therefore be more accurate to speak of Christian approaches (in the plural) to education, in the same way that we spoke of Christian approaches to spirituality. This rich diversity among Catholic schools is also helpful because it can provide a school with a stronger sense of its own distinct history and character and thus with a bulwark against erosion of its Christian ethos. Such distinctiveness is certainly worth defending.

Education: A short history of Catholic Schools in the UK

In the United Kingdom, prior to the nineteenth century virtually all schools were Christian in foundation and privately funded, but a series of initiatives in that century led to partial state funding and the creation of non-denominational schools run by local school boards. The nineteenth century also saw an increase in the Catholic population and the establishment of Catholic schools, many run by religious orders. From this mix, in 1902 the Balfour Act brought into one system the local board-schools, and voluntary Church of England and Catholic schools. Since this time the number of non-religious state schools in England has increased, but Catholic schools and Church of England schools together still comprise approximately one third of the state sector. In addition to these, schools in the independent sector (7% of schools in England) tend on average to be considerably older than local state schools, and the influence of Christianity is ubiquitous. Most have their origins in Christianity, and most continue to express this in the classroom and the school chapel. Despite the efforts of a small number of secularists to suppress state-funded Church schools, up to the present the sector has been supported by governments both on the 'right' and on the 'left', in part out of a recognition of religious diversity and the rights of parents, and in part out of a recognition that these schools are popular and successful (in worldly terms). For details of the current provision from the Catholic sector see *Catholic Education in England and Wales* 2014.

The Catholic school as a Communion

Since the sixth century, the Church has not abandoned its commitment to education and has continued to found and support Catholic schools. These schools are not only institutions used by the Church to fulfil her mission. The Catholic school is a communion, an expression of the Church.

The Catholic school is a communion, an expression of the Church.

According to the Second Vatican Council, the Church is to be understood first as the people of God gathered by God from every nation. More than a community she is a communion of persons sharing a common life, the life of the Holy Spirit, and constituting a living body, the body of Christ. Within this body not all have the same function, and some have the roles of leading, teaching or offering sacrifice. Nevertheless, the Church is not to be identified first with those who fulfil these official or priestly roles, but first in the unity of the people as a whole in Christ, as a communion.

Within Catholic theology there has been an increasing awareness in recent years that, as well as the universal Church throughout the world, the local church served by its priest is also an expression of this communion. In a related way, the Christian family is the 'domestic Church'. According to Paul in the Scriptures, when a Christian man and woman marry, their marriage is a mysterious sign of the union of Christ and the Church (Ephesians 5:22-23). The Catholic Church recognises the valid marriage of a baptised man and woman as a 'sacrament', an effective sign of the presence of God. The couple express this sacramental identity by the way they love one another, by praying together, and by serving others. If the couple are blessed with children, then the education of these children in the faith is also an expression of the family as Church, as the teaching Church. Thus when a family participates in their local church community they are a church within a church, or rather, the same Church (there is really only One Church throughout the world) but present in a different way.

The ecclesial church, the domestic church, and the teaching church.

A school is not simply an accidental gathering of people. Any school, inasmuch as it is a school, is a community of common purpose.

Something analogous can be said of the Catholic school. In the first place, a school is not simply an accidental gathering of people. Any school, inasmuch as it is a school, is a community of common purpose. If a school is to communicate to students a coherent understanding, a unified vision of the human person, then the different teachers must themselves share a common vision. Furthermore, as argued in the first part of the book, schools have an important role in supporting the development of the moral virtues, and this is communicated in part by the lives of teachers and their relationships within the school.

This understanding of the school as an educational community is important also for Catholic schools because 'that which does not reproduce the characteristic features of a school cannot be a Catholic school'. In addition to this, a Catholic school is, or ought to be, a community in a more profound sense. The Catholic school is a community gathered explicitly in the name of Christ and the unity of this community is given not only by common actions and a common purpose but because of a unifying and life-giving Spirit. In a word, the Catholic school is a *communion*, an expression of the Church, and especially of the teaching Church. The teaching Church is present in the teaching of the pope and bishops, and in a different way in the domestic church of the family which is the primary place of education. Nevertheless, as schools in general have an important role in education, so the Catholic school is also an important expression of the educating Church.

Section 3

This identity of the Catholic school as Church also shows itself in the way that the school is united with the parishes, chaplaincies and other expressions of the Church in the diocese in being under the care of the local bishop. The bishop exercises a ministry of leadership in the diocese and has responsibility to support the churches under his care. This care may express itself by recommending certain resources to support the curriculum or the ethos of a school. It also expresses itself through visitation of the school, which is an opportunity to express the relationship of the school not only with the diocese but with the universal church through the world.

Catholic secondary schools will generally have a relationship with Catholic primary schools and this relationship is not only practical but pastoral and religious. Helping ensure a good transition for students from primary to secondary is also helping to ensure that the virtues and vision fostered in the primary school take root in a new environment. The primary school gives the child into the care of another institution, in relationship to his or her educational needs, but if this is understood properly it will mean his or her human and spiritual flourishing. This can be helped by good communication between schools but also by some shared activities, including shared reflection on the Christian mission and ethos of the school.

While Catholic primary schools have links with Catholic secondary schools, and these have links with Catholic sixth form colleges, where these exist, there are few Catholic institutions of higher education in the United Kingdom, and most of those who go to University will go to a more or less secular institution. Furthermore, while most students from a primary school would go to one or two secondary schools, students at secondary schools would go to dozens of different universities. This makes it difficult to ensure continuity of spiritual care between school and university, even where the student wishes to deepen his or her understanding and practice of the faith. It would be helpful for schools to keep up links with the Catholic chaplaincies of different universities, just as they offer information about other aspects of those universities. It would be even more helpful were schools to encourage students to make contact with Catholic chaplaincies prior to arriving at university. This would provide students with a further place of support which could be of great comfort in their first days in a new environment, and also would ensure that chaplains could contact students to offer support and to let them know of activities.

Every approach to education presupposes an understanding of the human person and a Christian approach will be based on the understanding of the person as existing in communion, not only in relation to other people but in relation to God.

The identity of a Catholic school as an expression of the communion of the Church should also inform its approach to teaching. A spirituality of communion can become 'the living breath of the educational community' (*Educating Together in Catholic Schools* 16). Teaching is then understood as to persons by persons. Every approach to education presupposes an understanding of the human person and a Christian approach will be based on the understanding of the person as existing in communion, not only in relation to other people but in relation to God. Furthermore it is the vertical communion with God in Christ that shapes and sustains the horizontal communion with other people (*Educating Together in Catholic Schools* 8). This is why prayer is so important in sustaining the ethos of a school, as will be explored further below. Another important consideration, lest this account seem distant from the very imperfect experience of community even within Catholic schools, is that this communion is a work of grace overcoming sin. By the virtue of hope we can be confident that grace will ultimately prevail, but we know that at times people will fall into sin and this may prevent a school being a community even in the minimal sense of upholding justice. To call a school 'Christian' or 'Catholic' is therefore not to encourage pride in what is has been achieved, for pride goes before a fall. It is rather to direct us to the source of hope and communion, not in our own strength but in the grace of God.

The Catholic school as a collaborative community

If the school is an expression of the Church, a Christian community, a communion, what does this say about religious diversity within a Catholic school? How does the identity of the School as Church relate to the place in the community of those teachers or pupils who are Christians from different ecclesial communities or who are not explicit or believing Christians?

It is no part of Catholic identity to exclude children of parents who are not Catholic, where there are places for such children.

Missionary School, Swaziland

The system of Catholic schools in the United Kingdom was established to help Catholic parents fulfil their educational role. In this respect it is different in Catholic schools in those countries where schools were established as part of a missionary activity. A Catholic school in Japan or India might have few if any baptised pupils, but would still be Catholic in mission and ethos and, for example, might still expect pupils to participate in religious education and in communal prayers. This shows that the proportion of Catholics within a school need not affect its Catholic character. It is a matter of justice that Catholic children are not deprived of the possibility of a Catholic education, and thus that Catholic schools prioritise the needs of the Catholic community, but it is no part of Catholic identity to exclude children of parents who are not Catholic, where there are places for such children. Nevertheless, it is important in such cases that parents understand and accept the identity of the School and support the school in maintaining its identity and ethos.

There may be pastoral challenges in schools where a minority of children are non-Catholic. Efforts should be made to ensure that non-Catholic children are enabled to participate equally in school life and do not feel marginal. Equally, there may be Catholic schools in England and Wales where only a minority of pupils are practising

Catholics and the model of a missionary school may then be highly relevant. Without vigilance, such a situation could even create a counterproductive ethos where it is more difficult for pupils to practise their faith than it would be even in a secular school. This kind of malign influence could be even greater within the subculture of the peer-group, especially among those passing through adolescence who may see it as a badge of identity to rebel against the official religious identity of the institution. Perhaps the greatest challenge for a Catholic school is to find ways to support pupils who wish to explore and express their Catholic faith in a context where most pupils are Catholics by baptism but are not practising.

Perhaps the greatest challenge for a Catholic school is to find ways to support pupils who wish to explore and express their Catholic faith in a context where most pupils are Catholics by baptism but are not practising.

As explored in the first section of this book, every school will have an ethos, a set of more or less coherent, more or less overt beliefs, attitudes, and practices which constitute the character of that school. Every school faces the challenge of cultivating an ethos that supports the aims of education and in every school, teachers have an essential role in creating and sustaining that ethos. In the case of a Catholic school, the sustaining of its specific educational ethos will depend on a critical mass of teachers who understand and practise the Catholic faith. Ethos, if it means anything, must shape the whole school and the teaching of all subjects, not just parts of the school or curriculum. It cannot be left to a few teachers, to those in certain departments or who are more active in the Church on a personal level. There are, furthermore, some key positions that have a greater impact on the ethos of a school and in a Catholic school these must be filled by people of committed and informed faith. In England and Wales, the bishops require that the Head, Deputy Head, and Head of RE must be practising Catholics, while urging that preferential consideration be given to practising Catholics for all teaching posts (and nonteaching posts where there is a specific religious occupational requirement, such as school chaplain). For a Catholic school to prefer to appoint teaching staff who are practising Catholics is in no way unfair but is rather a matter of justice and is enshrined in law.

Every school will have an ethos, a set of more or less coherent, more or less overt beliefs, attitudes, and practices which constitute the character of that school.

Theology: Non-Catholic teachers in a Catholic school

What, then, is the place of non-Catholic teachers in a Catholic school? If a Catholic school is an expression of the Catholic Church, then not despite this but precisely because of this, it must be open to working collaboratively with Christians of different traditions and with all men and women of good will for the Common Good. Openness to such collaboration is mandated by the Second Vatican Council, which is binding on all Catholics. Indeed, according to the official teaching of the Church, Catholic education 'is not reserved to Catholics only, but is open to all those who appreciate and share its qualified educational project' (*The Catholic School on the Threshold of the Third Millennium* 16). The first part of this book aimed to show that the foundation of the Catholic vision of education is the dignity of the human person, the possibility of human flourishing, and the aim of integral formation in the moral and intellectual virtues. This foundation is something that can be acknowledged with or without commitment to any particular religion. The second part of the book showed what difference Jesus makes to the picture. It is a difference that marks out Christians, but it is not reserved to Catholics. Some ways of understanding the Church or the sacraments will be distinctive of Catholics, but many elements of the Catholic ethos will be shared by all the churches.

A Christian ethos marked by awareness of sin and grace, and inspiring hope for every child and for society, is one that can be appreciated and shared also by teachers who are not Catholic and who may not be explicitly Christian. Indeed, the task of cultivating and sustaining this ethos is one which should include all staff as a collaborative community. 'The virtues of all members of staff, non-Catholic Christians and those from other religious traditions make a valuable and treasured contribution to the quality of the school's Catholic life and ethos' (*Christ at the Centre* page 27).

The role of prayer

The Catholic life and ethos of a school should also be evident in and supported by the visible physical environment of the school. The Church, by its very essence, is the visible expression of God's grace, and this should therefore also be true of a Church school. Its ethos should be visible first in the way that a spirit of communion informs teaching, but also in the physical spaces within which staff and students learn and relate. Christians hold that, in Christ, the invisible God became visible for the sake of all humanity. This has inspired generations of Christian artists and architects and should be expressed in the physical environment of the school by images, statues, and crucifixes, and if possible, by a dedicated chapel within the grounds of the school. As well as making space for visible signs to remind staff and students of the presence of God in the school, it is important also that the school makes time to be mindful of God.

When students learn about God in classes on religion the question of God's existence is often framed in the third person. Students are encouraged to ask whether or not there is a God, whether the world is created and sustained by God for some purpose or whether it is somehow unmade and unsupported and has no purpose. They may learn about the arguments of the philosophers, Plato and Aristotle, Anselm and Aquinas,

God is not just an object to be referred to in the third person, or as an object of study, but is a Trinity of persons who engages with human beings as persons

Hume and Kant. God is regarded as an object of study, a conclusion of an argument, a being who might or might not be out there.

If the world is created, if my life and history as a whole has a direction and an ultimate purpose, this is certainly worth knowing, and if philosophy can help then it is certainly worth studying. However, the study of these kinds of questions, good and useful as it is, is not religion, at least not the Christian or the Jewish religion. The Scriptures show God not only as creating the world, but as speaking to human beings, and as the Word who is spoken and as the Spirit who inspires the prophets and inspires people to believe. God is not just an object to be referred to in the third person but is a Trinity of persons who engages with human beings as persons.

God is not just an object to be referred to in the third person but is a Trinity of persons who engages with human beings as persons.

A good example of this personal relationship is provided by Augustine of Hippo. As a young man Augustine was searching for some source of meaning or way of life, but it was only at the age of 32 that he became a Christian. This is how he expresses it in his autobiography where he thanks God for his conversion.

'Late have I loved you, O Beauty ever ancient, ever new, late have I loved you! You were within me, but I was outside, and it was there that I searched for you. In my unloveliness I plunged into the lovely things which you created. You were with me, but I was not with you. Created things kept me from you; yet if they had not been in you they would not have been at all. You called, you shouted, and you broke through my deafness. You flashed, you shone, and you dispelled my blindness. You breathed your fragrance on me; I drew in breath and now I pant for you. I have tasted you, now I hunger and thirst for more. You touched me, and I burned for your peace' (*Confessions*, X.27).

Augustine here talks not only of God but directly to God, and feels able to only because God has come into his life. It is not that he finds God but that God finds him. The relationship is initiated by God, by grace. God, as creator, and source of all that is good and beautiful, was always there; it was just that Augustine did not realise it. He was looking for God in the wrong places and it took God's action for Augustine to come to his senses.

A Catholic school ought to be not only a place to learn about God and Jesus Christ, but to a place to encounter God and hear the invitation of God to find ourselves in him. Schools, then, ought to be places of prayer and places where students discover how to pray. Learning starts by imitation and by common prayers: prayers at assemblies or at the beginning of lessons or at midday or before meals. The school ought also to provide support for teachers to learn to pray or to relearn this. Such support should also be offered to all staff, no matter from what background and what discipline. 'Opportunities for spiritual retreats should be provided for pupils and staff' (*Christ at the Centre*, A7.7). Even the agnostic can pray to a God who might be there and even an atheist can learn to be still and to be attentive to what is around and what is within. This can be a form of waiting on God. Indeed, cultivating the capacity to be still and to listen is fundamental to well-being in general as well as to the ability to pray.

Theology: What is prayer?

Prayer has been described as 'raising the heart and mind to God' (St John Damascene), and this is a good definition because it reminds us that within a relationship, the first requirement is to be aware of one another, to pay attention. However, the language of 'raising up' can be misleading if it implies that some people can raise their minds higher than others by their own efforts and that praying is a kind of performance where someone can become perfect. Only God is perfect and prayer is largely about being honest about our imperfections and our needs.

'Prayer is a practical recognition of God as the supreme being – the perfect one – the first cause, not merely of our being with its limitations, but of our redemption with its remedy for our imperfections and its strong helping-hand to new and eternal destinies' Vincent McNabb *Faith and Prayer*, page 141.

This definition is also helpful, as it makes reference to some specific ways of understanding God: as perfect, a first cause and as our Saviour. The old motto *lex orandi, Lex credendi*, (roughly, the law of what to believe is given by the law of how we should pray) – suggests that good prayer will depend on the way we understand God and our relationship to God. Hence the need for catechesis and for theological formation to support prayer, as well as provision of 'space' to pray.

Prayer is an expression of the virtue of hope, by which we relate our particular hopes and fears to God, principally by asking God for what we need or want. When Jesus taught his followers to pray he first told them to ask for things that they needed or wanted, 'Ask and it will be given you, seek and you will find' (Matthew 7:7). The theologian Herbert McCabe said that if we are distracted in prayer this is nearly always our real wants breaking in on our edifying but bogus wants. 'If you are distracted, trace your distraction back to the real desires it comes from and pray about these' (*God, Christ and Us*, page 8). Prayer is an expression of the virtue of hope, by which we relate our life, our hopes and fears, to God. We should pray for the world and for peace, but if what is bothering us is our job or a relationship, or even if we are thinking whether we can afford a new car, that is what we should pray about. Sometimes God gives us what we ask for; sometimes, for reasons we do not fully understand, God chooses to give us something else instead. However, the act of asking for what we want is

> Prayer is an expression of the virtue of hope, by which we relate our particular hopes and fears to God, principally by asking God for what we need or want.

an act of honesty, which is the beginning and bedrock of any relationship. If prayer is recognised as an expression of our needs and desires, not a mark of our perfection, then it may become easier for teachers to pray, and perhaps to begin lessons with a prayer.

From a Catholic perspective the source and summit of the life of prayer is the Mass or the Eucharist.

From a Catholic perspective the source and summit of the life of prayer is the Mass or the Eucharist. During the Mass the believer is united with that greater prayer, the self-giving of Jesus Christ to the heavenly Father. It is therefore essential to a Catholic school that Mass is celebrated, ideally in a dedicated space within the school itself. Those teachers or pupils who are not Catholics, including those who are not baptised, should be encouraged to attend and to use the opportunity to reflect and pray in the silence of their hearts. Those who are Catholics in good faith should be encouraged also to participate both by listening and praying and also by receiving communion. A school Mass is a celebration of the school as a communion.

Christian ethos across the curriculum

It is true of any school that the content of the curriculum reflects and shapes its ethos. The curriculum of the school implies a judgement about what is worth learning and about whether and how subjects interrelate with one another. This should be especially so in a Catholic school where all subjects can be related to a Catholic understanding of the human person and hence to one another.

An important contribution to education of a Catholic vision is precisely in helping defend the value of knowledge as such, as well as human skills and virtues.

A unified vision of education will include its historical dimensions, and the contribution of Christianity to the various different subject areas, as sketched out in the previous chapter. This sense of history can be applied to each of the disciplines and is one way in which subjects can be seen to be related to Christianity and to one another. However, such a Catholic *historical* perspective, while helpful, must be secondary to a Catholic *theological* account of the aims of education. While there is some merit in arguments of the form 'What have the Romans ever done for us?', at least as a corrective to secular attacks on Catholic education, such arguments risk obscuring the inherent value of each subject area. Indeed, an important contribution to education of a Catholic vision is precisely in helping defend the value of knowledge as such, as well as human skills and virtues. The Catholic Church therefore warns teachers not to consider other subjects 'as mere adjuncts to faith or as a useful means of teaching apologetics' (*The Catholic School* 39). Rather each, in its own way helps enable the pupil 'to assimilate skills, knowledge, intellectual methods and moral and social attitudes, all of which help to develop his personality and lead him to take his place as an active member of the community of man. Their aim is not merely the attainment of knowledge but the acquisition of values and the discovery of truth.' (*The Catholic School* 39)

Knowledge is a value because it is a fulfilment of the person who is to be understood in relation to other persons and the Common Good. This is made explicit in another quotation from the same Church document, 'Education is not given for the purpose of gaining power but as an aid towards a fuller understanding of, and communion with man, events and things. Knowledge is not to be considered as a means of material prosperity and success, but as a call to serve and to be responsible for others.' (*The Catholic School* 56)

The ethos of a Catholic school is the pattern of belief and practice of a learning community united in the conscious pursuit of the ultimate end of human life, revealed and made possible by Jesus Christ. The unifying principle of Catholic education, which should inform the whole curriculum, is thus the integral development of the human person, a person only properly understood in relation to other people and in communion with God. Education will therefore involve developing a student's self-understanding, both as a human person and as someone called to a communion with God made possible by Christ. So, for example, there will be a value in studying history for its own sake, as an intellectual discipline; this discipline will then have a further value in understanding more deeply the human person; and then there will be the Christian self-understanding that comes from considering the specific history of Christian people and institutions; and, finally, there is explicitly theological reflection on the meaning of historical events, both religious and secular. Considering each of these objectives will help identify which periods and which methods or approaches to include in the curriculum. The curriculum should include some explicitly religious themes but, in the first place, pupils should be 'encouraged to develop a taste for historical truth, and therefore to realize the need to look critically at texts and curricula which, at times, are imposed by a government or distorted by the ideology of the author'. (*The Religious Dimension of Education in a Catholic School* 58)

Similarly, study of literature should help students understand the power of narrative and the characteristics and possibilities of different genres, but literature also will be a means of understanding human life, and in addition to this there will be the specific contribution of Christian poets and novelists to the understanding of human life in relation to God (especially in relation to sin and grace). It should be evident that some examples of literature will be better or worse for understanding the art of writing, for understanding human life, and specifically for understanding human life in its religious dimensions. Literature will be good in different senses, for what it conveys and how it conveys it, and an aim of education will be to enable children to appreciate literature that is good in each of these senses. The ability to identify and love good literature is a gift for the whole of their lives, an aspect of human flourishing.

In relation to the physical sciences and the life sciences there will be an analogous development of the mind and of various intellectual virtues, and an analogous benefit in relation to knowledge and self-understanding, in this case understanding of the world in its physical reality. However, because the natural sciences abstract from reality and seek precise and characteristically quantitative knowledge of this or that aspect, they do not provide the resources to relate their conclusions to a vision of a whole. In order to recognise the place of the diverse scientific disciplines, as aspects of human understanding, students need to be introduced also to the history and to the philosophy of science. The work of relating the sciences to the unity of the human person is a philosophical task. Ideally this should be done in the context of studying the sciences themselves, not in a different class.

It is also the bane of contemporary education, and not only at school level, that people think only within their own discipline or subject area, and do not integrate their thought in a more holistic way. Overcoming this fragmented understanding is a fundamental aim of Catholic approach to education and ought to be a fundamental concern when designing the curriculum. In addition to choosing topics and approaches that will help students develop intellectual virtues, and which will help the students' self-understanding, schools need to provide opportunities for staff and students to relate disciplines to one another. This is not only a matter of relating other subjects to RE or to ethics (discussing the religious themes in Hamlet or the ethics of stem cell research) but more urgently of helping teachers (and thence students) see more generally how subjects can each be related to the other: the physics of music, the history of medicine, the politics of translation, the geography of art.

In such a way teachers themselves can learn to respect and to relate to the disciplines of others, and can begin to grasp the diversity of the intellectual virtues and the many-sided unity of the human person. A Catholic vision will see theology as the keystone of this united vision, but before disciplines can engage specifically with theology it is useful to learn what it is to engage with any other discipline. No subject area is self-contained and it is possible to attain a more complete understanding by interdisciplinary dialogue.

A Catholic school must therefore 'be committed to the development of a programme which will overcome the problems of a fragmented and insufficient curriculum. Teachers dealing with areas such as anthropology, biology, psychology, sociology and philosophy all have the opportunity to present a complete picture of the human person, including the religious dimension.' (*The Religious Dimension of Education in a Catholic School* 55)

9. The Mission of a Catholic School

Some pointers for making use of this chapter

This chapter sums up the vision of Catholic education provided in the book as a whole. It also contains some practical guidance on negotiating issues of cooperation in relation to fundraising /charity work, support for justice and peace and the integral principles of justice.

This chapter encourages schools to be proactive in making links with university Catholic chaplaincies, at the very least providing information about the activities of university chaplaincies and contact details for them for all those who are Catholic and who are preparing to apply to university. This could be a role for the school chaplaincy team but only if supported by the governors and senior management so that it is regarded as a normal part of preparing for university.

The theme of vocations to holiness could and perhaps should shape the provision of careers advice and again this could perhaps be enhanced by the involvement of the school chaplaincy team with 6th form careers week, though there may be other ways to stress this theme. At a deeper level the discussion of vocation relates to those aspirations that the school engenders and the vision of the good life it seeks to communicate. This may be a subject for INSET reflection among teachers and within departments as it goes to the very heart of the purpose of education.

Curriculum links

AQA

RS AS Unit H Religion and Contemporary Society (RSS08) (Faith schools)

RS A2 Unit 3F Religion and Contemporary Society (RST3F) (Faith schools)

The Church's mission to the world

The previous chapter related the ethos of a Catholic school to its identity as an expression of the Church. To understand the mission of a Catholic school it is therefore necessary to understand the mission of the Church. Indeed, this is true, to some extent, of any organisation. The very idea of an organisation having a 'mission', in the sense of a set of fundamental aims which might be expressed in a 'mission statement', is an idea that is derived from the Christian Church. It is the Church that expresses her identity in terms of 'mission' and other organisations have borrowed this terminology in an effort to express, or construct, their identity. The word mission means 'sent', and to understand it we need to understand first God as the one sending and God as the one sent.

The Church is the people of God gathered by God from every nation, and given a share of the life of the Holy Spirit to become the body of Christ. The people of God are gathered only because God first comes to them. This is what we mean by the grace of God, God's free gift to us of himself. Jesus understood himself as the beloved Son who had been sent into the world and who, together with the Father, sends the Spirit into the world, in order to bring people back to God. People need to be brought back to God because of sin, our individual sins and the sin of the world in which we share from the time we enter the world. Sin alienates us from God and from one another. Human beings are scattered and lost by sin but we are gathered together and found when God comes to us to bring us home.

As the Father sends the Son into the world and the Father and the Son send the Spirit, so Jesus sent his disciples into the world to be his ambassadors. This is how, in history, the Church was founded. Jesus gathered people during his lifetime to be his disciples and then, after his resurrection, he sent them out as apostles to spread the good news. The Church therefore, is not only the people who are gathered by God, but is also, at the same time, the people sent out by God, to bring God to others. Human life, the lives of individuals and of the whole human race, can thus be understood as a movement from God and a return to God. The Church is an expression of this movement and is both the people gathered in and the people sent out in the name of Christ. The Church has a 'mission' in that she is 'sent out' by Christ to complete his work, which is to bring salvation to the world, and to gather into one the whole human race in faith, hope, and love.

Within the Church there are some people who are 'missionaries' who are sent to regions where the Church is not well-established, to preach to those who have never heard the gospel and to plant new local churches. This missionary activity requires a lively faith and courage and the Church recognises, celebrates, and supports this work. The missionary work of the Church has continued in every age, and continues still. Without taking anything away from this, there is an important sense in which every Christian also shares in the mission of the Church. The Christian virtues of faith, hope, and love, and the gifts of the Spirit direct us to God and direct us to serve God by serving one another. This is our common mission.

> The Church has a 'mission' in that she is 'sent out' by Christ to complete his work, which is to bring salvation to the world, and to gather into one the whole human race in faith, hope, and love.

The mission of the Church is therefore to be of service to the world, and the nature of this service is twofold. In the first place the Church has a role in preaching the word so that people can understand their lives in relation to God. The world is created by God and the Spirit of God is able to touch the hearts of all people in ways we do not see, but there is also a gift we do see, when God gives people the faith to believe in Christ explicitly. This is a great gift that brings meaning into people's lives, hope based not on human strength but on God, and a share in the love of God. This essential aspect of the Church's mission is called, 'evangelisation', meaning the proclaiming of the 'good news' of our salvation by Christ.

'God is love, and he who abides in love abides in God, and God abides in him' 1 John 4:16

Section 3

In the second place the Church is directed by love to serve all people by acts of mercy, and to save and purify all that is good in the world. This mission of love includes affirming the dignity that human beings possess as created in the image of God. It includes engagement with culture and with society. It is not only that serving people, for example through education or healthcare, can be a way to witness to the faith, an indirect way of evangelising. Even apart from the value of good works in giving credibility to the Christian message, serving other people is itself an expression of Christian love. Serving others is what the kingdom of God looks like. 'God is love, and he who abides in love abides in God, and God abides in him' (1 John 4:16). Jesus showed this love in his life, death, and resurrection. He also left his disciples with a new commandment, 'that you love one another; even as I have loved you' (John 13:34).

'that you love one another; even as I have loved you' (John 13:34).

Justice animated by love

The aspect of the Church's teaching most directly concerned with this mission of Christian love is called Catholic social teaching. In its modern form this dates back to a series of encyclicals (public letters to the whole Church) by Popes. The first in

this series was 'Of New Things' (generally referred to by its Latin title *Rerum Novarum*) promulgated by Pope Leo XIII in 1891, which looked at the rights and duties of workers and the owners of capital. Another important source for this teaching is the Second Vatican Council especially its 'Pastoral Constitution on the Church in the Modern World' (also known as *Gaudium et Spes*).

Mother Teresa of Calcutta

Documents on Catholic Social teaching

Rerum Novarum (On the Condition of Labour) - Pope Leo XIII, 1891

Quadragesimo Anno (After Forty Years) - Pope Pius XI, 1931

Mater et Magistra (Christianity and Social Progress) - Pope John XXIII, 1961

Pacem in Terris (Peace on Earth) - Pope John XXIII, 1963

Gaudium et Spes (Pastoral Constitution on the Church in the Modern World) Vatican Council II, 1965

Populorum Progressio (On the Development of Peoples) - Pope Paul VI, 1967

Octogesima Adveniens (A Call to Action) - Pope Paul VI, 1971

Justicia in Mundo (Justice in the World) - Synod of Bishops, 1971

Laborem Exercens (On Human Work) - Pope John Paul II, 1981

Solicitudo Rei Socialis (On Social Concern) - Pope John Paul II, 1987

Centesimus Annus (The Hundredth Year) - Pope John Paul II, 1991

Deus Caritas Est (God Is Love) - Pope Benedict XVI, 2005

Caritas in Veritate (In Charity and Truth) - Pope Benedict XVI, 2009

Section 3

The Church's rich social teaching is one of the greatest treasures of the Catholic tradition, but throughout history many Christians have neglected it and have focused only on personal spirituality or on the more individual aspects of morality. For this reason Catholic social teaching has sometimes been called 'the Church's best kept secret'.

'So God created man in his own image, in the image of God he created him; male and female he created them' Genesis 1:27

The starting point for Catholic social teaching is the *dignity of every human being* as made in *the image of God*: 'So God created man in his own image, in the image of God he created him; male and female he created them' (Genesis 1:27). The dignity of the human person is the basis of all human rights and freedoms. The creation of every human being in the image of God is a reason to respect one another, but it is not a reason for pride, for the book of Genesis also tells the story of the fall. The Christian story is not an untroubled journey of human dignity and achievement but is a drama of sin and grace, of loss and gain. In a Catholic understanding, the dignity that is there in every person is sometimes hidden or wounded by sin; but Jesus showed God's love for human beings even when we sin.

After the human race lost its original justice human beings became jealous of one another and then turned to violence. This idea is expressed in the Bible in the story of Cain and Abel. Cain kills his brother, Abel, because he is jealous of him. When God asks Cain where his brother is, Cain replies 'I do not know; am I my brother's keeper?' (Genesis 4:9). This saying is ironic, because it is precisely as brothers and sisters of fellow human beings that we have a responsibility for one another. *Solidarity* is the recognition of the common bond that exists between individuals and between peoples. The word solidarity helpfully reminds us that love in its Christian sense is not so much the act of helping a stranger out of our generosity but is recognising a brother or sister who demands our help and respect.

'I do not know; am I my brother's keeper?' Genesis 4:9

Just as, by solidarity, we recognise the bonds between persons, so the Christian understanding of the Common Good is that the good of society is neither the sum of individual goods nor is it a social good that fails to respect the dignity of persons. The Common Good is the good of society understood precisely as a communion of persons with one another and with God. The Common Good implies that the community has a common duty to ensure that everyone is provided for, but it does not imply that no-one can have their own private property. Catholic teaching is that God created the earth for the benefit of all people, and none should be excluded. This is sometimes called the doctrine of 'the universal destination of goods'. However, the Church recognises that there are virtues in allowing people to hold property for themselves and their families, as this encourages stewardship, rewards labour, and enables people to show hospitality to one another. It follows from this that private property is acceptable within due social limits, but always for the sake of the Common Good. The right to hold property cannot be an absolute and thus the community can and should redistribute wealth and should also hold some goods communally. While people should be given opportunities to exercise solidarity with one another by acts of voluntary charity, the selfish tendency of human sin is such that private initiatives alone cannot be relied on to answer human need.

As the Common Good respects the dignity and interdependence of persons, it also respects the dignity of different levels of community between the individual and the state. This is especially true of the family, which is a fundamental building block of society, but it is also true of schools, businesses, and voluntary associations of various kinds. The principle of *subsidiarity* is that all power and decision-making in society should be at the most local level compatible with the Common Good. For some kinds of decision it is right that they are made at a high level, by national law or international agreement. However, many decisions are best made by local communities or associations and it is an injustice to take these decisions away from local people. Sometimes failures at a lower level will be used as an excuse radically to extend the power of the highest level of government, for example by state regulation of the media, of education, or of the family. This is to forget that the root source of harm, which is human sin, exists at the centres of power just as much as it exists at the grass roots. There will be failures at every level and so there should be checks and balances in any system, each informed by good sense and by the virtue of hope.

The sins of individuals and groups distort society so that injustices are perpetuated and hard to remedy because of what Pope John Paul II called 'structures of sin'. To resist the effects of these historic and ongoing injustices it is necessary to make a specific commitment to those who suffer injustice and whose perspective is systematically marginalised in society. This is what the Church terms the *preferential option for the poor*. Every human being, rich or poor, has dignity, deserves respect, has material and spiritual needs, but the gospel requires Christians to think first of those who might be overlooked. It makes the poor its priority.

The school as a community of justice & love

The first principle of Catholic social teaching is the dignity of the human person, and thus the first test for any institution as a community of justice and love is how it expresses, or fails to express, respect for the dignity of everyone it affects. This will include pupils and staff, both teaching and support staff. It will also include parents, school governors, people who live nearby and others whom the school encounters in one way or another. The school as an employer will have various statutory duties to those who work at the school, and may be subject to further requirements from local authority, the diocese or previous agreements between management and staff. It may have limited scope for making decisions about matters such as pay and conditions, particularly if it is in the voluntary aided state sector. Nevertheless, where the school has control over these matters the question is whether it acts only for the economic interest of the institution or whether it takes account of Catholic teaching with regard, for example, to a just wage or to the rights of workers' associations. Schools may benefit from help of unpaid volunteers, but where a wage is paid, justice and not merely legal or economic requirements should determine its level.

Another area of social teaching which is challenging for any organisation is the degree to which patterns of decision-making are informed by the principles of solidarity and subsidiarity. How are decisions made, and to what extent do staff and parents participate in decision making? There is sometimes a tension between the quickest or most efficient way to make a decision, and the way that most involves those who should be involved. Democracy is notoriously inefficient, and subsidiarity certainly does not require every institution to run by popular votes. However, in a Christian community, where people are affected by decisions and can reasonably participate, they should have a role in the process. It is not unusual for there to be tension between different schools, or between parents and a school, or between a school and the local diocese, over issues such as reorganisation, amalgamation, selling or building property, or making use (or not making use) of new legal frameworks for school status. While authority in the local Church rests ultimately with the bishop, the principle of subsidiarity implies that parents and teachers have a key role in these decisions.

An aspect of the justice of institutions that particularly affects schools is the safeguarding of children from abuse or physical assault and the protection of staff from assault and from false accusation. A greater awareness over recent years of sin in this area and of concomitant safeguarding issues has led to the development of policies and procedures, some of which may be experienced as very onerous, such as those for potential volunteers. If such policies are to be effective and are to be embraced it is essential that they are, and are seen to be, aimed at protecting vulnerable individuals, rather than regarded primarily as protecting the institution and its reputation. This applies in particular to the investigation of accusations so that risk to the vulnerable is minimised but the principle of the presumption of innocence is maintained. Justice and solidarity also requires the safeguarding of staff.

Part of justice is freedom from discrimination, harassment or bullying behaviour, and so the school should have in place general policies to prevent such behaviour, whether among children, or among staff or between staff and children. It is also important to discourage gossip and the vices of detraction, backbiting, and tale-bearing, even though such behaviour is an issue in any small community. Thus it is unacceptable to allow a child to be bullied or picked on because he is a Muslim in a majority Christian School. On the other hand it is unreasonable for the child or his parents to complain that they are offended by the public display of Christian symbols, or the expression of Christian beliefs. The Catholic school has a duty and thus a right to be true to its Christian mission and ethos.

In relation to equality and diversity among staff, it is entirely reasonable for a Catholic school to expect staff not to contradict Catholic teaching, for example on matters such as sexual ethics, and not to object if Catholic doctrine is taught in a Catholic school. This will require, at very least, some commitment not to act in a way that publicly contradicts the ethos of the school. At the same time, policies in relation to the witness of staff to the ethos of a Catholic institution should not intrude unreasonably on the proper scope of private life of those working in that institution. A due respect for privacy is enshrined not only in secular law but in the Church's own law, 'No one may unlawfully harm the good reputation which a person enjoys, or violate the right of every person to protect his or her privacy' (Canon 220).

An important expression of the mission of a Catholic school in relation to love and justice are activities such as participation in parish and local voluntary work and raising money for institutional charities, especially but not only Catholic charities. Such activities have a rightful place in any school. They are formative for generosity and responsible citizenship. In a Catholic school these actions will be given a particular emphasis and care should be taken also in relation to the kinds of charities that are supported. Giving to charity should not be about 'feeling good' but about 'doing good' and hence should be informed by good sense, including asking how money is spent and what good it does. Some charities will have aims, or use means, that contradict respect for human dignity – such as those that fund or promote abortion or population control or sexual liberation, or research charities that fund selection of, or experiments on, human embryos. It would be wrong for a Catholic school to support these charities. Instead, the school should seek other ways to address the good aims of the charity (where such good aims exist); for example, by supporting alternative charities in the same sector.

School charity event - sponsored walk

Schools may also have to think carefully about contributing to large umbrella campaigns. For a number of reasons it is generally preferable to support a small number of charities directly, rather than a broad campaign with diverse purposes. Large umbrella causes (such as *Comic Relief*) may put a distance between the donor and the end beneficiary (aside from questions that might be asked about the nature of some of the recipient charities). This distance, while not bad in itself, removes control from the giver and risks making the precise reasons for giving less clear. More direct approaches to charitable giving, such as through twinning relationships, exchanges, and support for particular projects, provide much greater educational value, and greater human value in solidarity.

If a Catholic school is a community of love and justice, embodying a preferential option for the poor, this will also have an impact on its admission policy. As stated

Section 3

above, it is not contrary to justice or to the gospel for individual schools to specialise and for some schools to take students who are stronger academically or to serve those Catholics whose parents can pay for their education. They also have needs. However, the particular concern for the Church as a whole should be for the poor and marginalised. The priority for the Catholic education sector therefore should be to assist those parents who desire a Catholic education for their children but who are socially marginalised by poverty, by linguistic or other barriers, or because their children have special needs. Repeatedly in the history of the Church, institutions established especially to provide for the poor have become so successful that they become the preserve of the rich. This is a 'counter-witness' (*The Catholic School* 58) to the Church's priority in education which is 'caring for the needs of those who are poor in the goods of this world or who are deprived of the assistance and affection of a family or who are strangers to the gift of Faith' (*Gravissimum Educationis* 9). The preferential option for the poor within education is a challenge with which the Church has struggled at least since the Middle Ages. It was already evident in the requirement that Cathedral churches make special provision for 'poor children who cannot be helped by the support of their parents'.

'caring for the needs of those who are poor in the goods of this world or who are deprived of the assistance and affection of a family or who are strangers to the gift of Faith.' *Gravissimum Educationis* 9

Vocations to holiness

The Catholic school is a place of education and, as such, shares not only in the Church's mission of love and justice but also in its mission of evangelisation. The Catholic school should be a place where pupils encounter the good news and have an opportunity to reflect on it. The first teachers of children are their parents and it is Christian parents who have the first duty to educate their children in the faith. Nevertheless, as the school exists to assist parents in the task of educating, so the Catholic school should assist parents in the work of nurturing the faith. Where parents are not baptised, or belong to a different ecclesial community, or are Catholic but do not practise the faith, the school should not evangelise overtly without the parents' permission, but should seek parental permission to be able to give children the opportunity to hear the good news.

An important element of this good news, especially within the context of a school, is that God has a particular concern for every person and each one has a path that God has prepared for him or her. The mission of a Catholic school will include helping pupils to interpret 'their existence in the light of God's plan' (*Consecrated Persons and their Mission in Schools*, 55, also *Christ in the Centre* A7.8) and to discern the path to which God is calling them. It is noteworthy that, just as the word 'mission' was used first for the mission of the Church and later adopted by secular organisations, so also the word 'calling' or 'vocation' (which is just the Latin word for calling) has also gained a secular use. Sometimes the word vocation is used simply to mean someone's profession or occupation, as for example with 'vocational education' which prepares people for specific trades, crafts or occupations. What is lacking in this secular sense is precisely the identity of the one who 'calls'.

helping pupils to interpret 'their existence in the light of God's plan'
Consecrated Persons and their Mission in Schools, 55, also *Christ in the Centre* A7.8.

To support someone trying to discern her vocation is very different from offering careers advice. At best, someone seeking careers advice is looking for generic information about how to pursue this or that desire. There is a sense of aptitude and desire but no sense of a specific calling. At worst the goal of a career could be framed exclusively in relation to attaining status through successful competition. This could then lead to a narrow focus on attaining grades or other requirements only as the doorway to a particular career, itself understood only as the doorway to wealth or social success. Such a focus would increase the pressure on teachers and on schools to hit targets in relation to grades at the expense of the aims of education. It would also increase the incentive for students to plagiarise or to cheat in other ways in order to secure the necessary grades. Grades would have become simply a means to an end.

Pope Francis warns that even those who hold or express a firm Christian faith may nevertheless 'frequently fall into a lifestyle which leads to an attachment to financial security, or to a desire for power or human glory at all cost, rather than giving their lives to others in mission' (*Evangelii Gaudium* 80). In contrast, a vocation in the Christian sense is not only an occupation but is the response to a call from God to serve others in a particular way. It is ordered towards service, but it is also particular to an individual, discerned by the gifts of the spirit and founded on the virtue of hope. It is because we believe that this is what God has in mind for us that we can have the courage to commit ourselves to a particular way of life. For many the nature of this path will be obscure for many years, and even where it seems clear, it always will involve twists and turns that are known to God alone. Nevertheless, the seeds of vocations for later careers, dreams, relationships, are often sown at an early age. It is never the case that we know all that God has in store for us, but we can be confident that God has some role for each of us by which we can come to him. A vocation understood in this way is not external to education and, while it might rely on grades, the results of our honest efforts in assessments will be part of how our vocation is discerned. It is part of the process of listening.

> A vocation in the Christian sense is not only an occupation but is the response to a call from God to serve others in a particular way.

As a vocation is a calling is from God, it is an aspect of a more fundamental vocation to find happiness through friendship with God. The Second Vatican Council expressed this fundamental vocation as the universal call to holiness. 'The Lord Jesus, the divine Teacher and Model of all perfection, preached holiness of life to each and everyone of His disciples of every condition. He Himself stands as the author and consumator of this holiness of life: "Be you therefore perfect, even as your heavenly Father is perfect"' (Vatican II Lumen Gentium 40). There is a universal calling to follow Christ, to be

Section 3

holy, to serve God in this life, and be happy with God forever in the next. Each person has a unique vocation through which he or she shares in this universal call.

'The Lord Jesus, the divine Teacher and Model of all perfection, preached holiness of life to each and everyone of His disciples of every condition. He Himself stands as the author and consumator of this holiness of life: "Be you therefore perfect, even as your heavenly Father is perfect"'

Vatican II *Lumen Gentium* 40

Supporting a sense of vocation in students will include encouraging them to be open to a vocation to religious life, as a religious sister or brother, and open to a vocation to the priesthood. It is difficult to discover such a vocation without seeing examples of such ministry, and schools should seek to broaden the spiritual experience available to students through offering retreats and pilgrimages and experiences of the Church in other contexts and other countries. It is good to invite people into school to explain their way of life and prayer so that students' imagination is opened to the many paths there are in life, secular and religious, and so that they can have an opportunity to hear a specific call if it comes for them. Such occasions should not be understood as exercises in recruitment or advertising (as though even these vocations were reduced to the 'milk round' of graduate careers). They should first be an occasion to learn of the works of God in the Church and an opportunity to listen. As it is only God who gives faith, it is only God who can call someone to a specific vocation, and some roles, including that of priest or religious, can only be undertaken with this sense of vocation.

Pilgrimmage doubling as a school retreat and vocation discernment

'Splendid therefore and of the highest importance is the vocation of those who act in the name of the community in undertaking a teaching career'.

Vatican II, *Gravissimum Educationis*

Among the vocations that pupils may consider is the vocation to be a teacher. Given the understanding of education set out in this book, teaching is not only a vocation to holiness, as every honest way of life is capable of being, but it is a visible ministry of the Church. Thus the Second Vatican Council says 'Splendid therefore and of the highest importance is the vocation of those who act in the name of the community in undertaking a teaching career'. The Catholic school is a communion which should embody a Christian ethos and fulfil a Christian mission. Teachers, of subjects across the curriculum, have an essential role in maintaining this ethos and carrying forward this mission. This gives them a responsibility to develop their own understanding of the faith and of the Christian understanding of education, which itself relies on a Christian understanding of the human person. Fulfilling the role of a teacher requires a commitment to professionalism: regularly refreshing skills and updating knowledge. It also requires keeping a lively awareness of vocation and of God's providence, so as to maintain a commitment to education in the face of the pressures that distort its significance.

Christ the beginning & end of education

The current context of education is dominated by a relentless pressure on schools to achieve measurable results. The bottom line seems to be grades attained, which translate to places on preferred courses at preferred universities, and which, it is imagined, will translate into entry into enviable graduate careers. Not all students or parents aspire to such a goal, but it is sufficiently widespread to shape the culture. This culture in turn shapes the curriculum, the regularity and predominant methods of assessment, and thus, the default methods of teaching. The curriculum is increasingly fragmented and incoherent. Assessments are frequent and are increasingly broken into units of information which students can be coached to reproduce. Education can then be reduced to teaching to the assessment.

'characterised by depersonalisation and a mass production mentality'
The Catholic School 31

In every age education is influenced by the culture of wider society, and in the modern world this is a society 'characterised by depersonalisation and a mass production mentality' (*The Catholic School* 31). Within this culture, the paradigm for thought is technical reasoning about means to an end. Furthermore, the ends validated by this culture are those desires that can be stimulated by advertising and can be satisfied by becoming consumers, customers, or clients.

This is a caricature but it contains enough truth to be recognisable and uncomfortable. The danger for Catholic schools is that rather than resisting these cultural pressures, schools strive to be successful according to measures that distort the true aims and ethos of education. Without conscious effort, the religious dimension of the school would then be reduced to the content of Religious Education classes and to certain external signs of identity.

'that which does not reproduce the characteristic features of a school cannot be a Catholic school' *The Catholic School* 25

In the face of such adverse cultural pressures, the immediate task of the Catholic school is therefore simply to be a school, for 'that which does not reproduce the characteristic features of a school cannot be a Catholic school' (*The Catholic School* 25). The primary mission of the Church to the world is to make known the person of Jesus. At the same time the Church has a duty 'to foster and elevate all that is found to be

Section 3

true, good and beautiful in the human community' (*The Church in the Modern World*, § 76). As an expression of this broader mission in love, the Catholic school should be a place where humanity is served through education in knowledge, skills and virtues, especially to those who are socially marginalised. Indeed, Christian teachers should be more keenly aware of the danger of fragmentation of human understanding due to sin, and of the tendency to subordinate knowledge to the search of power or prestige.

'to foster and elevate all that is found to be true, good and beautiful in the human community' *The Church in the Modern World*, § 76

A key aspect of the mission of the Church is therefore to help humanise education, seeking or restoring a unity of vision. A Catholic school should acknowledge the importance of education for the transmission of culture and the economic benefits of education to pupils and to society. However, at the same time the school should encourage students to be critical of elements of culture or aspirations of society where these are not 'subordinated to the integral perfection of the human person, to the good of the community and of the whole society' (*The Church in the Modern World*, § 59).

not 'subordinated to the integral perfection of the human person, to the good of the community and of the whole society' *The Church in the Modern World*, § 59

The first section of this book set out certain elements of education that fulfil human persons and which could, in principle, be known to natural reason. These include: the dignity of the human person, the concept of human flourishing, the integral formation of the human person by the virtues, the primacy of learning over teaching, the primary role of the parents in education, and the development of the mind as a fundamental aim of a 'liberal' education. A true education will seek to overcome the fragmentation of the curriculum and will retrieve an idea of the human person that is holistic and universal. All these elements should be acknowledged within a Catholic understanding of education.

Going beyond this, but without neglecting anything that is good and true in a natural account of education, a Christian account will be based on the person of Jesus who reveals the ultimate end of human life and who is the way to that end. Christian education is the integral formation of the human person in the conscious pursuit of his or her ultimate end and of the ultimate good of the society as revealed and made possible by Jesus Christ. It is only in the mystery of Jesus Christ that the mystery of the human person is fully revealed and thus,

> Christian education is the integral formation of the human person in the conscious pursuit of his or her ultimate end and of the ultimate good of the society as revealed and made possible by Jesus Christ.

'Christ is the foundation of the whole educational enterprise in a Catholic school' (*The Catholic School* 34). The revealed story of sin and grace explains why it is so difficult to attain a unified vision of the human person, while giving us hope that such unity is possible, because it is seen in the person of Christ. The Christian vision will not nullify the idea of virtue, but will transform our understanding of the virtues and of what characteristics count as virtues.

'The Christian model, based on the person of Christ, is then linked to this human concept of the person - that is, the model begins with an educational framework based on the person as human, and then enriches it with supernatural gifts, virtues, and values - and a supernatural call.' Congregation for Catholic Education *The Religious Dimension of Education in a Catholic School 1988*

'Christ is the foundation of the whole educational enterprise in a Catholic school' *The Catholic School 34*

The theological virtue of hope has a special place in relation to education which looks towards the future. Hope is expressed and exercised especially in prayer through which we submit our desires and fears to God. Hope transforms the virtue of good sense so that, as well as considering the probability and desirability of events, we have confidence that our life is in the hands of God. Every person has a particular 'supernatural call' and a path that God has in store through which a person can find friendship with God and become holy. Pupils should be encouraged to recognise the care God has for each person and helped to discern what their vocation might be. This in turn should affect the way in which they approach life in school, studies, the stresses of assessments, and the uncertainties of the future.

Pantocrator

'We do not prepare our boys for life. We prepare them for death.'

The headmaster of a well-known Catholic school is once said to have remarked 'We do not prepare our boys for life. We prepare them for death.' This remark was perhaps deliberately shocking and paradoxical and we should resist the opposition implied. Christianity is about life and death, and the resurrection of the dead. Nevertheless, this quotation points to something profound. Even the best naturalistic account of education is limited to this world. Education understood only in relation to natural reason is the formation of the person as a free being with those intellectual and moral dispositions which will enable him or her to flourish in this life. In contrast, Christian education is the development of the person in relation to her ultimate end. Catholic education must therefore introduce students to the *momento mori*. It must aim to help students develop an understanding of themselves as human persons created in the image of God, alienated through sin but rescued by grace, who each have a particular vocation to serve God and others in this life, until, entrusting their souls to Christ in death, they can be united with him and with the whole people of God in the life of the world to come.

Section 3

Definitions

Art: The word 'art' at its broadest refers to the skill of making something well so that it is useful and/or beautiful. [chapter 7]

Christ: The word 'Christ' is the Greek equivalent of the Hebrew word 'Messiah' meaning 'the anointed one' and refers to the promised Saviour who would be King of the Jews and heir to the throne of David. [chapter 4]

Conscience: Our conscience is our capacity to make considered judgements recognising the moral quality of an action. [chapter 2]

Courage: Courage is the disposition that enables us to act well in the face of what is arduous or dangerous. [chapter 2]

Culture: The word 'culture' comes from cultivation of the soil but has come to mean the development of mind and especially its artistic and intellectual development and the human achievements that have followed from this. [chapter 6]

Discernment: Discernment is the process by which someone discovers the path to which he or she is being called by God. [chapter 5]

Disposition: A disposition is an acquired inclination to act and to react in certain ways. [chapter 1]

Education: Education is the integral formation of the human person, through the cultivation of the moral and intellectual virtues, for the good of the person and for the common good of society. [chapter 3]

Education (Christian): Christian education is the integral formation of the human person in the conscious pursuit of his or her ultimate end and of the ultimate good of society as revealed and made possible by Jesus Christ. [chapter 9]

Ethos: Ethos is the pattern of belief and practice of a community that embodies and expresses its fundamental dispositions and objectives. [chapter 3]

Ethos (Christian): The ethos of a Catholic school is the pattern of belief and practice of a learning community united in the conscious pursuit of the ultimate end of human life, revealed and made possible by Jesus Christ. [chapter 8]

Faith: The theological virtue of faith is the gift of God which enables us to place our trust in God and to believe what has been revealed as a word from God. [chapter 5]

Friendship: Friendship in its highest or truest sense is shared personal life constituted by an equal and mutual relationship of unselfish love. [chapter 1]

Good sense: Good sense is the virtue that informs our practical decisions, when they are made well. [chapter2]

Gospel: The Gospel is the 'good news' that, through the death and resurrection of Christ, God has reconciled the world to himself, has overcome sin and death, and has sent the Holy Spirit among us to bring us eternal life. [chapter 4]

Grace: The word 'grace' means 'free gift' and refers to the help we receive freely from God. It refers especially to the gift by which we live well and by which we become friends of God. [chapter 4]

Holiness: Holiness is the effect of the Holy Spirit in a human person to make someone 'holy', which means, 'set apart' for the service of God. [chapter 4]

Hope: The theological virtue of hope enables us to face our own future and that of the whole world with the confidence that God has prepared a path for each of us through which we can come to happiness. [chapter 5]

Human Flourishing: Human flourishing is the aim of human life and consists in the shared enjoyment of emotional, cultural, intellectual and spiritual life and, in particular, the sustaining of true friendships. [chapter 3]

Incarnation: The Incarnation is the word Christians use to reflect the mysterious truth that, in Jesus, God became human, without ceasing to be God and without overwhelming his humanity. [chapter 4]

Justice: Justice is the disposition of our will (our rational appetite) which inclines us to give each person his or her due. [chapter 2]

Literature: We give the name 'literature' especially to narratives or well-crafted phrases which express well some significant human meaning. [chapter 6]

Love: The theological virtue of love or charity is that gift of God that enables us to love God with the love of true friendship and to love others as God loves us. [chapter 5]

Mission (of the Church): The Church has a 'mission' in that she is 'sent out' by Christ to complete his work, which is to bring salvation to the world, and to gather into one the whole human race in faith, hope, and love. [chapter 9]

Persons: Persons are capable by nature of relating to one another as 'I' to 'you'. Human beings are persons in virtue of being, by nature, rational animals. [chapter 1]

Prayer: Prayer is an expression of the virtue of hope, by which we relate our particular hopes and fears to God, principally by asking God for what we need or want. [chapter 8]

Providence: Providence is the care and foresight by which God provides for the world and humanity so that things are able to achieve their end. [chapter 5]

Revelation: Revelation is the knowledge that creatures can have of God based on a word that God has spoken to them. [chapter 4]

Religion: The virtue of religion is the disposition of a rational creature to acknowledge and honour the Creator. [chapter 6]

School: Schools are places of learning established to assist parents in the education of their children by providing access to specialised knowledge and skills and to the cultural legacy of previous generations. They also provide a context to learn social virtues, so that by learning together, pupils also learn to be together. [chapter 3]

Secularism: Secularism when it becomes an ideology, what is sometimes called 'programmatic secularism', involves suppressing all expression of religion in the public sphere and thus effectively imposes a form of state atheism on all citizens. In contrast an older and more tolerant form of 'procedural secularism' allows access to the public sphere to those of all faiths and none and thus protects free speech and conscience both for individuals and institutions. [chapter 6]

Science (the Natural sciences): The natural sciences (that is, the physical and the life sciences) employ various forms of observation, experiment, and mathematical analysis in order to attain precise and characteristically quantitative knowledge of physical reality. [chapter 7]

Sin: Sins are actions that are incompatible with the love of God and they are deadly (or 'mortal') inasmuch as they cut us off from the life that comes from God. [chapter 5]

Sin (original): The primeval alienation from God into which each of us is born. [chapter 5]

Sin (venial): An act that fails to express love but which is trivial or excusable. [chapter 5]

Soul: The word 'soul' refers to the principle of life, the form or actual organisation of a living being. [chapter 1]

Spirituality: The word spirituality, in a Christian sense, is the transforming effect of the Holy Spirit upon the person as the person makes his or her way to God by the way that is Christ. [chapter 4]

Temperateness: Temperateness is the disposition that enables us to act and react well in the face of what is desirable. [chapter 2]

Tolerance: Tolerance is the virtue of respecting the freedom of others to be themselves within the context of a shared understanding of the common good. [chapter 2]

Vice: A vice is a settled disposition to do the wrong thing, or to do the right 'external' thing but in the wrong way. [chapter 2]

Virtue (moral): A moral virtue is a settled disposition to react in the right way and do the right thing; that is, to do what promotes the true flourishing of human persons. [chapter 2]

Virtue (intellectual): The intellectual virtues are those dispositions of the mind that enable a person to reason well and to come to a knowledge of the truth. [chapter 3]

Vocation: A vocation in the Christian sense is not only an occupation but is the response to a call from God to serve others in a particular way. [chapter 9]

Bibliography

Magisterial documents on education (listed chronologically). These texts are all available online via the Vatican website: http://w2.vatican.va/content/vatican/en.html

Pius XI *Divini illius magistri* 1929

Vatican II Declaration on Christian Education *Gravissimum educationis* 1965

Congregation for Catholic Education *The Catholic School* 1977

Congregation for Catholic Education *Lay Catholics in Schools: Witnesses to Faith* 1982

Pope John Paul II '*Address to Catholic educators*' 12 Sept 1984

Congregation for Catholic Education *The Religious Dimension of Education in a Catholic School* 1988

Pope John Paul II '*Address to Teachers and Students of the Catholic Villa Flaminia Institute*' 23 February 1997

Congregation for Catholic Education *The Catholic School on the Threshold of the Third Millenium* 1997

Congregation for Catholic Education *Consecrated Persons and their Mission in Schools* 2002

Congregation for Catholic Education *Educating Together in Catholic Schools (A shared mission between consecrated persons and the lay faithful)* 2007

Pope Benedict XVI '*Address to Catholic educators*' 17 April 2008

Congregation for Catholic Education *Letter to the presidents of bishops' conferences on religious education in schools* 2009

Catholic Bishops' Conference of England and Wales Department of Catholic Education and Formation *Religious Education Curriculum Directory* 2012

Congregation for Catholic Education *Educating to Intercultural Dialogue in Catholic Schools: Living in Harmony for a Civilization of Love* 2013

Congregation for Catholic Education *Educating Today and Tomorrow: A renewing passion (Instrumentum laboris)* 2014

Catholic Education Service and Catholic Bishops' Conference of England and Wales *Catholic Education in England and Wales* 2014

Other relevant magisterial documents

Pope Pius XII *Humani Generis* 1950

Vatican II *Lumen Gentium* (Dogmatic Constitution on the Church) 1964

Vatican II *Gaudium et Spes* (Pastoral Constitution on the Church in the Modern World) 1965

Pope Paul VI *Populorum Progressio* (On the Development of Peoples) 1967

Pope John Paul *Catechesi Tradendae* Apostolic exhortation 16 October 1979

Code of Canon Law 1983

Congregation for the Doctrine of the Faith *The Truth and Meaning of Human Sexuality* 1986

Catechism of the Catholic Church Second edition 1997

Works cited in the text (listed alphabetically by author)

For works published after 1900 a current publisher and date, and the original publisher and date, are provided. All works published prior to 1900 are available online and generally also in a number of different print editions.

Adams, R., *Watership Down* (Puffin 2012, originally Rex Collings 1972)

Anscombe, G.E.M., *Human Life, Action and Ethics,* edited by M. Geach, L. Gormally (Imprint Academic, 2005)

Aquinas, Thomas, *Summa Theologiae*

Aristotle, *De Anima*

Aristotle, *Metaphysics*

Aristotle, *Nicomachean Ethics*

Augustine, *Confessions*

Bede, *Ecclesiastical History of the English People*

Chesterton, G.K. *The Common Man* (Sheed and Ward 1950)

Chesterton, G.K., *Heretics* (Wilder Publications 2009, originally John Lane Company 1905)

Chesterton, G.K., *Orthodoxy* (Ortho Publishing 2014, originally John Lane Company 1908)

Dante (Durante degli Alighieri), *Divine Comedy*

Department for Education, *Statutory guidance National curriculum in England: framework for key stages 1 to 4* (updated 16 July 2014) available online

de Sales, Francis, *Introduction to the Devout Life*

Eusebius of Ceasarea, *Ecclesiastical History*

Golding, W., *Lord of the Flies* (A & A Publishers 2013, originally Faber and Faber 1954)

John of Damascus, *On the Divine Images*

McCabe, H., *God, Christ and Us* (Continuum 2005)

McNabb, V., *Faith and Prayer* (Blackfriars 1953)

McNabb, V., *Where Believers May Doubt* (Blackfriars 1903)

Miller, W.J., *A Canticle for Leibowitz* (HarperCollins 2006, originally J. B. Lippincott & Co. 1960)

Newman, J.H., *The Dream of Gerontius*

Newman, J.H., *The Idea of a University*

Orwell, G., *Animal Farm* (Penguin Classics 2000, originally Secker and Warburg 1945)

Republic, Plato

Puzo, M., *The Godfather* (Arrow 2009, originally G. P. Putnam's Sons 1969)

Schumacher, E.F., *Small is Beautiful* (Hartley and Marks 2000, originally Blond & Briggs 1973)

Scruton, R., *Understanding Music* (Continuum 2010)

Stock, M., *Christ at the Centre: Why the Church provides Catholic schools* (Catholic Truth Society 2012)

Tolkein, J.R.R., *Lord of the Rings* (HarperCollins 2007, originally George Allen & Unwin 1954-1955)

White, A.D., *The Warfare of Science with Theology in Christendom* [1896, available online. NB that this work is seriously inaccurate; for criticisms see main text and see below under further reading: science and religion]

Williams, R., 'Statements, acts and values,' in S. Prickett and P. Erskine-Hill (ed.) *Education! Education! Education!* (Imprint Academic 2002)

Further reading

Catholic education

The texts listed below do not all take the same view of Catholic education but represent a critical discourse involving different perspectives. Multiple perspectives are also represented in journals such as *International Studies in Catholic Education* and *The Journal of Catholic Education* (formerly *Catholic Education: A Journal of Inquiry and Practice*).

Arthur, J., *The Ebbing Tide: policy and principles in Catholic education* (Gracewing 1995)

Arthur, J., H. Walters, and S. Gaine, *Earthen Vessels: The Thomistic tradition in education* (Gracewing 1999)

Grace, G., *Catholic Schools: Mission, markets and morality* (Routledge 2002)

Haldane, J. 'Chesterton's philosophy of education,' *Philosophy*, January 1990: 65-80.

Hanvey, J. and A. Carroll, *On The Way To Life* (Heythrop Institute for Religion, Ethics and Public Life, 2005)

Lydon,J., (2013), 'Teaching as a Vocation'; 'Religious Charism in Salesian Schools'; 'Faith and the Catholic Teacher'; and 'The Nature of Spiritual Capital' in *The Pastoral Review* Vol. 7(5); Vol. 7(6); Vol. 8 (5); and Vol. 9 (5) respectively.

Maritain, J., *Education at the Crossroads* (Yale University Press 1943)

Miller, J.M., *The Holy See's teaching on Catholic Schools* (Sophia Institute Press 2005)

Morris, A.B. (ed.) *Catholic Education: universal principles, locally applied* (Cambridge scholars 2012)

Morris, A.B. (ed.) *Re-imagining Christian education for the 21st century* (Matthew James 2013)

O'Donoghue, P., *Fit for Mission? Schools* (Lancaster Roman Catholic Diocese, 2007)

Storr, C., *Serving Two Masters? Catholic school governors at work* (Gracewing 2011)

Christianity

Pope Francis, *What is the Church?* (Catholic Truth Society 2014)

Ivereigh, A., *How to defend the Faith without raising your voice* (Huntington, OSV Press, 2012)

Jones, D.A., *Christianity: An Introduction to the Catholic Faith* (Catholic Truth Society 2012)

O'Collins, G. and M. Farrugia, *Catholicism. The Story of Catholic Christianity* (Oxford University Press 2004)

McCabe, H., *God Matters* (Mowbray 2006)

McCabe, H., *The Teaching of the Catholic Church: A New Catechism of Christian Doctrine* (Darton, Longman & Todd 2000)

Pinsent, A. and M. Holden, *Apologia: Catholic Answers to Today's Questions* (Catholic Truth Society 2010)

Radcliffe,T., *What is the Point of being a Christian?* (Continuum 2005)

Ratzinger, J., *An Introduction to the Catholic Faith* (Catholic Truth Society 2012)

Ratzinger, J., *Christianity* (Ignatius Press 2004)

Sheed, F. *Theology and Sanity* (Sheed and Ward 1953)

Youcat: The Youth Catechism of the Catholic Church (Catholic Truth Society 2011)

Ethics

Bishops' Conference of England and Wales *Cherishing Life* (Catholic Truth Society 2004)

Fisher, A., *Catholic Bioethics for a New Millennium* (Cambridge University Press 2011)

Jones, D.A., *Living Life to the Full: An Introduction to Christian Morality* (Catholic Truth Society 2013)

Jones, D.A., *The Soul of the Embryo* (Continuum 2004)

MacIntyre, A., *Dependent Rational Animals: Why Human Beings Need the Virtues* (London, Duckworth, 1985)

Mattison, W., *Introducing Moral Theology: True Happiness and the Virtues* (Brazos Press 2008)

McCabe, H., *The Good Life* (Continuum 2005)

Pieper, J., *Four Cardinal Virtues* (University of Notre Dame Press 1966)

Schönborn C. *Living the Catechism of the Catholic Church* Volume 3: Life in Christ (Ignatius Press 2001)

Watt, H. *Life and Death in Healthcare Ethics* (Routledge 2000)

Watt, H. (ed.) *Cooperation, Complicity and Conscience: Problems in healthcare, science, law and public policy* (Linacre Centre 2005)

Watt, H. (ed.) *Fertility and Gender: Issues in reproductive and sexual ethics* (Anscombe Bioethics Centre 2011)

Science & Religion

Carroll, W.E., *Creation and Science* (Catholic Truth Society 2011)

Carroll, W.E., *Galileo: Science and Faith* (Catholic Truth Society 2009)

Barr, S.M., *Modern Physics and Ancient Faith* (University of Notre Dame 2006)

Ferngren, G., *Science & Religion: A Historical Introduction* (Johns Hopkins University Press 2002)

Gould, S.J., *Dinosaur in a Haystack: Reflections in Natural History* (Crown 1996)

Jaki, S., *The Road of Science and the Ways to God* (University of Chicago Press, 1978)

Midgley, M., *Evolution as a Religion: Strange Hopes and Stranger Fears* (Routledge Classics 2002)

Pinsent, A. and M. Holden, *Lumen: The Catholic Gift to Civilisation* (Catholic Truth Society 2011)

Sullivan, D.J., *An Introduction to Philosophy: perennial principles of the classical realist tradition* (TAN 2009)

Index

Picture credits

[Title page] *Baldachin*. Inside the Interior of the Saint Peter Cathedral Basilica. Vatican City, Rome, Italy. © Cesc Assawin/Shutterstock.com

[Page 12] *St Gregory the Great Roman Catholic Secondary School*, Oxford. © James & Taylor Dynamic Façade Solutions

[Page 13] *Father Herbert McCabe* OP. Courtesy Peter James Hunter

[Page 16] *Cheshire cat*. From Alice's Adventures in Wonderland original vintage engraving. © Morphart Creation/Shutterstock.com

[Page 17] *Sunrays over young seedling*. © Tagstock1/Shutterstock.com

[Page 20] *Camera lens aperture* © Akirbs/Shutterstock.com

Beagle puppy active playing with stick at the beach. © Soloviova Liudmyla/Shutterstock.com

[Page 22] *Piggy in tweed suit with walking stick*. © Olga Angelloz/Shutterstock.com

[Page 28] Left to right:
1. *Temperance*. By Piero del Pollaiolo. From a series of panels depicting the Virtues designed for the Council Chamber of the Merchant's Guild Hall. © Galleria degli Uffizi, Florence, Italy/ Bridgemanimages.com

2. *Prudence*. By Piero del Pollaiolo. From a series of panels depicting the Virtues designed for the Council Chamber of the Merchant's Guild Hall. © Galleria degli Uffizi, Florence, Italy/Bridgemanimages.com

3. *Fortitude*. By Botticelli, Sandro (Alessandro di Mariano di Vanni Filipepi) From a series of panels depicting the Virtues designed for the Council Chamber of the Merchant's Guild Hall. © Galleria degli Uffizi, Florence, Italy/Bridgemanimages.com

4. *Justice between the Archangels Michael and Gabriel*. By Jacobello del Fiore. © DEA/A. Dagli Orti/ gettyimages.co.uk

[Page 28] *Chariot with gladiator* © Voropaev Vasiliy/Shutterstock.com

[Page30] Logo from the *The Godfather* film.

[Page 37] *Elizabeth Anscombe*. © Stephen Pyke/ Gettyimages.com

Great White Shark Body. © Catmando/Shutterstock.com

[Page 42] *Plato and Aristotle composite*. Plato statue at Athens Academy © Yoeml/Shutterstock.com. *Aristotle*. By sculptor Marinali © PPL/Shutterstock.com

[Page 44] Father and son fishing. © G-stockstudio/Shutterstock.com

[Page 49] Diagram 1. *Jean Piaget's Theory of cognitive development* © CTS.

[Page 50] Diagram 2. *Benjamin Bloom's Taxonomy of educational objectives*. © CTS.

[Page 51] Diagram 3. *Lawrence Kohlberg's Stages of moral development* © CTS.

[Page 58] *Stars and nebulae* © Viktar Malyshchyts/Shutterstock.com

In the beginning. © Alistair Scott/ Shutterstock.com

[Page 61] *Jacob wrestles with the angel*. © Nicku/ Shutterstock.com

[Page 62] *Psalm 23* © Christophe Testi/Shutterstock.com

[Page 64] Symbolic representations of Matthew, Mark, Luke and John. *Christ and four saints*. Altar panel designed by Burne-Jones, Thomas Rooke Matthews. © Private Collection, Photo: Bonhams, London, UK/Bridgemanimages.com

[Page 66] *Mother and Child*, stained glass in Vatican Museum, Rome, Italy. © Aykutkoc/Shutterstock.com

[Page 68] *John the Baptist baptising the Christ*. By John Nava. The Cathedral of Our Lady of the Angels, Los Angeles, California, USA © Photo: Supannee Hickman/Shutterstock.com

[Page 70] Left to right: 1. *The Ecstasy of St Teresa of Avila*. By Gian Lorenzo Bernini, Church of Santa Maria della Vittoria, Rome, Italy. © Photo: Dea/G. Nimatallah/getty images.co.uk.

2. *St Benedict statue*. In the grounds of Ampleforth Abbey. © Photo: Lawrence Lew, OP

3. *San Juan de la Cruz* statue. © Photo: Lawrence Lew, OP

[Page 72] *St Maria Goretti*. Stained glass of the martyr. © Zvonimir Atletic/Shutterstock.com

[Page 73] Nietzsche. From Meyers Lexicon books © Nicku/Shutterstock.com

[Page 75] *Cain slaying Abel*. Le Sainte Bible: Traduction nouvelle selon la Vulgate par Mm. J.-J. Bourasse et P. Janvier. Tours: Alfred Mame et Fils. 2) 1866 3) France 4) Gustave Doré © Ruskpp/Shutterstock.com

[Page 77] *Sinking Saint Peter and Jesus Christ walking on the water*. Stained glass window in St. George's Anglican Cathedral, Perth, Australia. © Tupungato/Shutterstock.com

[Page 79] *Dog looks hopefully for its walk*. © Javier Brosch/Shutterstock.com

[Page 81] *Tobias with the archangel Raphael and fish scene*. Part of The Miracle fishing triptych. By Peter Paul Rubens in church of Our Lady across de Dyle, Mechelen, Belgium. © Photo: Renata Sedmakova/ Shutterstock.com

[Page 82] *The Last Supper*. Detail from a medieval alabaster carving in the British Museum, London, UK. © Lawrence Lew, OP.

[Page 85] *Professor Stephen Hawking*, London. © David Fowler/Shutterstock.com

[Page 88] *Opening of Parliament attended the religious leaders of the country*. Kiev, Ukraine © IgorGolovniov/Shutterstock.com

[Page 91] *St Augustine of Hippo*. Mosaic in front of the church on the Mount of Beatitudes. © Zvonimir Atletic/Shutterstock.com

[Page 95] *Right Reverend Dr Rowan Williams*. © Mark William Penny/Shutterstock.com

[Page 101] *Fr Lemaitre and Albert Einstein*. Los Angeles, California, USA © Bettmann/Corbis

[Page 103] *Nikolaus Kopernicus*. From Meyers Lexicon books © Nicku/Shutterstock.com

[Page 106] *Painting of Pentecost scene from the cathedral in Antwerp, Belgium*. © Renata Sedmakova/ Shutterstock.com

[Page 111] *Bartolome de las Casas of America*. Chromolithography. © Leemage/Corbis

[Peg 112] *Madonna with Child and two angels*. Zagreb, Croatia © Zvonimir Atletic/Shutterstock.com

[Page 113] *Two Afghan girls with flowers*. Keshim, Badakhshan, Afghanistan. © Lizette Potgieter/ Shutterstock.com

[Page 114] *Gospel choir sings anthems*, at Halifax Rainmen. © Matthew Jacques/Shutterstock.com

[Page 117] *King's School Canterbury*. © Photography Victor Naumenko/PictsofEngland.com

Gate of St Augustine Abbey, Canterbury, Kent, UK. © Route66/Shutterstock.com.

[Page 118] *St Francis De Sales statue*. From the chapel of the Salesianum in Rome. © Photo: Lawrence Lew, OP.

[Page 118] *Don Bosco statue*. © Photo: Lawrence Lew, OP.

[Page 121] Picture to illustrate different kinds of 'communion' (1. ecclesial, 2. domestic, 3. educational). Left to right:

1. *Priest with church members families*. © Mazur Photography.
2. *Happy family at dinner*. © Monkey Business Images/Shutterstock.com.
3. *Students in class*. © Areipa.lt/Shutterstock.com.

[Page 123] *Unidentified Swazi schoolboys*. Nazarene Mission School, Piggs Peak, Swaziland. © Pal Teravagimov/Shutterstock.com.

[Page 126] *Antique Russian Orthodox icon*. The Old Testament Trinity. Veliky Novgorod, Russia. © FotograFFF/Shutterstock.com.

[Page 133] *Teresa of Calcutta feeding someone*. Postage stamp printed in Italy. © Catwalker/ Shutterstock.com.

[Page 137] *Group of young people in an urban landscape*. © Artens/Shutterstock.com.

[Page 140] *WYD Pilgrims*. St Dominic's priory. © Lawrence Lew, OP.

[Page 143] *Christ Pantocrator*. 13th century Deesis Mosaic of Jesus. Hagia Sophia Museum, Basilica in Istanbul, Turkey. © Faraways/Shutterstock.com.